To my parents:

Dad, who gave me the gift of questioning,

and Mom, who believed in infinite possibilities

How Big Is Your God?

The Freedom to Experience the Divine

Paul Coutinho, SJ

LOYOLAPRESS.
A JESUIT MINISTRY
Chicago

LOYOLA PRESS.
A JESUIT MINISTRY

3441 N. Ashland Avenue
Chicago, Illinois 60657
(800) 621-1008
www.loyolapress.com

Scripture taken from the HOLY BIBLE, NEW INTERNATIONAL
VERSION. Copyright © 1973, 1978, 1984 International Bible Society.
Used by permission of Zondervan Bible Publishers.

Cover design: Judine O'Shea
Cover photo: Roine Magnusson/Stone/Getty Images
Interior design: Maggie Chung

Library of Congress Cataloging-in-Publication Data
Coutinho, Paul.
  How big is your God? : the freedom to experience the divine / Paul
Coutinho.
    ISBN–13: 978-0-8294-2481-2
    ISBN–10: 0-8294-2481-4
  1. God—Christianity. 2. Spiritual life—Christianity. 3. Spirituality.
I. Title.
    BT103.C69 2007
    231—dc22

                                                                 2007014416

First paperback printing: August 2010
paperback ISBN–13: 978-0-8294-3294-7, ISBN–10: 0-8294-3294-9

Printed in the United States of America
10 11 12 13 14 15 Bang 10 9 8 7 6 5 4 3 2 1

Contents

viii

Introduction

Organized religion appears to be coming to a significant impasse in many parts of the world. It amounts to "a new reformation," but, more important, a new *kind* of reformation. No one seems too interested in forming yet another Christian break-off group or new denomination. That would be too easy, too old, and too futile. Whether we fully realize it or not, we are learning from many of our past mistakes, and our spiritual desire is moving deeper. You are surely about to experience that here!

What I see emerging is quite simply a desire for authentic God experience—instead of mere external belief systems, about which we can be right or wrong. People do not feel they have to leave their existing group, call its beliefs into question, or overreact to any particular part that they do not yet understand or agree with. They just quietly move toward a much deeper renewal of encounter at levels of prayer, inner experience, spiritual disciplines, and various kinds of contemplative practice.

This marvelous book by Fr. Paul Coutinho is an excellent example of this new and Spirit-led direction. He does not allow you to hide in your head behind any preexisting conclusions but instead invites you on a journey where you know something for yourself. The something that you come to know is so good, broad, and deep that it keeps you from wasting time on anything negative, self-protective, or reactionary. Finally, what one discovers is not something at all, but Somebody.

After three different preaching tours in India over the years, I have come to agree with the common refrain that "no Westerner visits India and comes back without being changed at a deep level." It is almost like meeting not just another hemisphere, but also another hemisphere of your brain and your soul. Fr. Paul is able to bridge these different worlds by his own Western education, his Jesuit and Christian spirituality, and his simple faithfulness to that uniquely Indian mind. I am convinced that the Asian mind is less dualistic than ours and is often able to present profound truths in a disarmingly clear, humble, and truthful way. We Westerners saw it in Anthony de Mello, Bede Griffiths, and Mother Teresa. You will see it here for yourself in Paul Coutinho.

The human ego hates a genuinely new experience. It hates to change and is preoccupied with control. We prefer ideas. We can do anything we want with a new idea, including agreeing with it too quickly. But a genuinely new experience does something with you! It leaves you out of control for a while and forces you to reassess your terrain, find new emotions, and realign your life coordinates. It is often a bit of a humiliation, because it upsets your old coordinates. We prefer to stay inside our small comfort zones and actually avoid any genuinely new experiences. The ego almost does not allow them to happen.

Now, if that is true in general, and I think it is, then imagine how much more so if we speak of God experiences!

Talk about being out of control. We tend to be well-armored against authentic God experience, because it always leads us into the unfamiliar, that new terrain where we are not in control and God is. St. Augustine said, "Si comprehenderis, non est Deus": "If you can understand it, it is not God." I guess that is why God usually has to break in or break us down to break through to us. We try to pull God into our little minds and worlds, when this big God is trying to pull us into a much bigger world, which we, almost by nature, resist. Jesus called it "the kingdom of God."

So I encourage you to trust this fine teacher and let him lead you to some very big and new places so that you too can experience what "no eye has seen, no ear has heard, no mind has conceived . . . what God has prepared for those who love him" (1 Corinthians 2:9).

You are in for a treat, and a treat that will last!

—Fr. Richard Rohr, OFM
Center for Action and Contemplation
Albuquerque, New Mexico

Author's Note

I'd like to begin with a brief introduction. There are three important things you need to know about me: I am Catholic, I am a Jesuit, and I come from India. My last name is Coutinho, which is Portuguese. You may be wondering how my Indian family got a Portuguese name and became Catholic. Well, let me tell you.

About four hundred years ago, the Jesuits came to India, traveling with Portuguese military explorers. They came to colonize us, baptize us, and bring us the Good News. They had a simple program for us. While young Jesuit scholastics-in-training were stationed on the outskirts of our village, the soldiers herded all the people into the center of the village, where they had to make a choice between being baptized and being killed. If you chose to be baptized, a Portuguese official would claim your soul for God and give you his last name. The Jesuits held mass baptisms and got rid of those who refused to be baptized, because at that time they firmly believed that there was no salvation outside the church. The Portuguese, on the other hand, found baptism to be an effective means of social and political control.

So, generations ago, my family and many Indians were baptized as Christians. But, of course, we Indians already had a rich and highly developed religious tradition that stretched back over two thousand years, and that tradition and its influences continue in India today. We were baptized but not really converted. This is why many Catholic Indians, like me, express our Christianity a little differently from others.

I am also a Jesuit priest, and most of what I believe about spirituality comes from my living exposure to Eastern religions and, above all, from holy Scripture and the spirituality of St. Ignatius of Loyola—especially *The Spiritual Exercises*, a small book written by St. Ignatius that is regarded as a great classic of Western spirituality. St. Ignatius, founder of the Jesuits, writes in the beginning of *The Spiritual Exercises* that the Exercises are all about using any means to experience God and deepen our relationship with the Divine. Find *your* way to experience God, St. Ignatius would say, and grow in *your* relationship with *your* God. He believed that our experience of and relationship with God is unique, and so your God is not my God, and my God is no one else's God. Now, St. Ignatius, being a Catholic saint, obviously believed in one God—one God, but infinite possibilities. Ignatius's point is don't deepen your relationship with the God your theology professor talks about; don't deepen your relationship with the God your mom talks about; don't deepen your relationship with the God society or even the church talks about. Deepen your relationship with the God you know, right now—the God who is constantly calling you into deeper union and communion. God is personal. God is unique. *God is an experience of the divine.*

One of my students once told me that her parents were "religious," but she did not see a personal relationship with God in their lives. That's a sad statement to make, and perhaps all too common for many of us. Do we have a relationship with God—or just a comfortable religion empty of divine experience?

While St. Ignatius was not particularly interested in teaching religion or doctrine, he did want us to have an experience of the Divine. After a life-shattering spiritual experience of God on the banks of the river Cardoner in Manresa, Spain, he wrote that even if there were no Scriptures to teach us, he would be resolved to die for what he had experienced at Manresa. Ignatius was ready to die for his experience of the Divine, and this experience became the absolute criterion for all the decisions he made for the rest of his life. Manresa also became his foundational experience, through which all the rest of his graces would deepen until he found himself in the divine being and essence.

Now, there are some smart, nice, and holy people who choose never to seek to experience the Divine. Why? Maybe it is because they do not know about these experiences, or, worse still, they have been told that such experiences are available only to a chosen few, like John of the Cross or Teresa of Ávila, and not to sinners like us. Or, deep down, they are held back by the false fear that if they become mystics, they will have to stop enjoying life: *The only way to meet God is through a kind of dying to self and letting God be God so that I can live the fullness of this life.* Or, if they do seek to experience God, they seek only a small God, a God manageable by their own standards. This is a limited God that the self—the clingy ego—won't feel threatened by. Unfortunately, with a small God, the response of these nice people to the world often becomes one of fear, anxiety, and helplessness, because when they are in need, their small God can do very little for them.

I invite you now to ask yourself: Am I looking to meet a *big* God, a God without limits? Do I have the will to experience the Divine—in all its wondrous and infinite possibilities?

If so—or if you're at least curious about meeting a big God—let's start our journey together where St. Ignatius would start: by questioning our lives, questioning the world around us, questioning our relationships, questioning our family life, questioning our work, and questioning our passions. Let's also question our relationship with God.

My hope is that this small book will inspire your desire for a greater and greater experience of the Divine, and that it will help you ask the right questions—the really important, life-and-death questions. Some things in this book might immediately make a lot of sense to you; other things might immediately confuse you. Still other things might make you feel uncomfortable or even cause you to recoil. And that's okay. My hope is that, over time, this book will also point you toward experiencing the Divine through experiencing your personal God. Such a journey takes courage, patience, and a good degree of surrender. Are you ready for such a quest? This is a big journey; it's the biggest journey we can make. But we can do this together—in fact, we can only do it together.

Are you ready?

How Big Is Your God?   1

Do you know God? Have you seen the face of the Divine? I like to tell people that the sum of life is our journey to find our identity in the Divine. But I think sometimes the only way to really say what I mean is to tell it in a story:

With Christmas coming, Grandma was out shopping for gifts for her grandchildren. While she was at the toy store going through her list and carefully selecting gifts, she noticed a small homeless girl outside wistfully looking into the store. Grandma's heart went out to this little girl. She invited her into the store and asked her to pick out a gift for herself. As they walked out of the store, the little girl held Grandma's hand and looked into her kind eyes and asked, "Are you God?" Grandma, somewhat embarrassed and somewhat touched, said, "No, my dear, I am not God." "Then who are you?" continued the little girl. Grandma thought for a moment and said, "I am a child of God." The little girl, fully satisfied and smiling, said, "I knew there was a connection."

When people come into your life, do they see a divine connection in you?

The little girl in the story had given Grandma a wonderful Christmas gift that day—a gift better than any gift Grandma would ever give or receive for the rest of her life. She realized her true identity as a child of God.

St. Paul tells us that when we believe that we are children of God, we become divine heirs (Romans 8:16–17), and the gifts of God are not our privilege—they become our *right*.

When people come into your life, do they see a divine connection in you?

How big is our inheritance? It will depend on how big our God is—it will depend on how big and infinite a God we allow ourselves to experience and come to know. "When [God] appears, we shall be like him, for we shall see him as he is" (1 John 3:2). As our God becomes bigger, so do we.

Do You Have the Will to Experience a Big God?

Once when I lived in the United States and was working as a chaplain at a hospital, I was called to the bedside of a man who was afraid of dying. When I got there, I saw his family around him and thought, *He must be afraid of dying because he's afraid of leaving his family behind to fend for themselves.* But this was not the case. And I would have understood if he was afraid of dying because he had things to do and places to go, but that was not the case either. This man was afraid of dying because he was afraid of meeting God. And do you know what? This man had made *forty-five* spiritual retreats. I have often wondered since then what kind of God was talked about in those retreats if after forty-five of them this man was afraid of dying because he was afraid of meeting God! How big was his God?

That same week, I was called to the bedside of a woman who had been given three days to live. When I went to visit her at Barnes-Jewish Hospital, she said, "Thank you for coming, Father. I was waiting for you. You know, before you came to visit me at the retirement home, I was afraid of God. I was afraid of his judgment and his punishment. After you came, I developed such a wonderful experience of and relationship with God that I cannot wait to die. I cannot wait to die, so that I can be with God." I realized at that moment that I was in the presence of a true mystic. A simple, faithful, everyday Catholic now turned genuine mystic.

Now, it's one thing to preach about dying and meeting God, but it's quite another to meet a person who is living out what is preached. And so, to break the tension of the moment, I said, "You know, when you go up there, just put in a good word for me." "Oh, Father," she said, "I am waiting to tell God everything about you." "Well," I said meekly, "please, not *everything*."

So we joked a little and I prayed with her, thanking God for such a beautiful life, for all the gifts that she had received and the opportunities God had given her to share those gifts with others, bringing peace, joy, love, and meaning to the lives of so many. We thanked God for the people who had come into her life, made a difference, and helped her feel worthwhile and happy. I know the world is a better place just because she lived in it. That night she died peacefully—not afraid of dying, because she wanted to be with God. A simple woman whose faith and devotion to Jesus and Mary opened her heart and brought her to the feet of a merciful God, who was waiting to celebrate her when she arrived in the divine presence.

When I share these two experiences with priests and religious across the globe, it is amazing to me how many of the senior men and women tell me that they belong to the first category. They are afraid of dying because they are afraid of meeting God. They are afraid of God's judgment and punishment. They are afraid because they are nearing the end of their lives and they hardly know God. They seem stuck with a belief in a small God that keeps them confined to a Good Friday Jesus and does not allow them to explore the God who rose on Easter Sunday. And they cry desperately for help!

More recently, two prominent retreatants at one of our Jesuit retreat houses complained, saying, "We came to the retreat house to be spiritually nourished, not to be spiritually challenged."

This is something we need to consider: Do we go to retreats, go to church, attend seminars and conferences, pray, and read books on faith to be spiritually nourished? Or do we do these things to be spiritually challenged?

The people of Israel understood this challenge of faith well. In the book of Deuteronomy, Moses recalls them saying, "Let us not hear the voice of the Lord our God nor see this great fire anymore, or we will die" (18:16). They knew that listening to the voice of God meant death. Seeing his holy face (the "great fire") is an invitation to die to our selfishness. It is a challenge to transcend the 1 percent of the world that is physical and move toward the 99 percent that is spiritual.

Then there is the rather humorous passage in Exodus where the people of Israel come to Moses and say, "Speak to us yourself and we will listen. But do not have God speak to us or we will die" (20:19).

So we go to our religious services and make sure we read the latest popular inspirational books and attend all kinds of psychospiritual wellness retreats and conferences. And we come away feeling good. But without the willingness to be spiritually challenged, we cannot and will not change. Without the will to give up whatever is asked of us in order to meet a bigger God, we find that our understanding and experience of the Divine cannot and will not grow.

Try taking that to your prayer and meditation time, and see what happens. Take this kind of willingness into the prayers you pray in the stillness and silence of your heart, and you will be seduced by God, just like Abraham was. Abraham was asked to leave behind everything he knew—his country, his kindred, his culture, and his belief in many gods—and was promised "a land flowing with milk and honey" (Exodus 3:8)

Without the will to give up whatever is asked of us in order to meet a bigger God, we find that our understanding and experience of the Divine cannot and will not grow.

and progeny that would be "as numerous as the stars in the sky and as the sand on the seashore" (Genesis 22:17). God invited Abraham to follow him through the desert to this new land. In this land, Abraham would experience a new way of living and would discover a bigger God. With this new relationship with God, Abraham would become a blessing wherever he went.

God took Abraham through the desert, and if you have the will to follow, he'll take you through the desert too. The desert represents a place of purification and pure encounter with God, with no obstacles or distractions. The desert is the place where you will experience the naked truth of who you are—the image and likeness of God, the divine breath. While you're in the desert,

God may come for your beloved Isaac and ask you to sacrifice him. Isaac was Abraham's son and God's own gift and promise to him.

Do you still want to know God? Do you still want to see the face of the Divine? Do you have the will to experience your own spiritual and divine identity and become a channel of divine blessing?

3 Are You Ready?

One Sunday while watching television, I happened on a gospel channel and heard a preacher tell his listeners that he had an important question for them. Now, I may not always agree with all that television preachers say, but I find them to be animated speakers, and I was curious to hear his question. The question was three words: "Are you ready?" He continued, "Are you ready when the Lord comes? Because when the Lord comes, he will not ask you whether you were in church today or not. When the Lord comes, he will not ask you whether you are a good Christian. He will not ask you about the great and admirable things you did in life. When the Lord comes, he will ask, 'Did you know me?'" And instead of changing the channel, I had to stop and reflect a moment, because this is something that I might have said—or would like to have said.

"Are you ready?" "Did you know me?" Do you know God? Have you seen the face of the Divine?

These are scary questions, because for many of us, religion is going to church. Many of us will want to answer, "I am ready, because I attend church every Sunday and keep all the commandments . . . well, except a few." But that is not the question that the Lord will ask. He will ask, "Did you know me?" "Have you seen the face of God?" "Have you experienced the Divine?"

Meister Eckhart, the great medieval mystic, believed that everyone needs religion as a well to take them to the river of God's love and divine life. This is a wonderful analogy. Wells are fed by rivers of life-giving water, but how often the well—and not the water it can provide—becomes the goal of our lives. Since we are seeking a big God, let's ask ourselves: has the well become the goal of our lives?

It often does. We fortify our well; we decorate it and adorn it with elaborate and beautiful liturgies; we say, "Look at our well. Look at what we've done and how wonderful it is." And we are never taken to the river. The purpose of the well is to take us to the river. The river gives us freedom and salvation. Everyone needs religion, yes. Religion is a means to freedom, but it is not an end in itself. Religion helps us find the river of life and the river of freedom, and it's in the river that we experience the love of God and divine life. A question we must ask ourselves is once we find the river, once we are experiencing the divine love, do we still need the well? Once Paul found the river in his Damascus experience, did he still need the Mosaic law?

Many of us settle for the comfort and security of the well without realizing that the river exists. One of my students once told me that her parents are good people—they go to Mass every Sunday and live by the laws of the church. Their well runs deep. It is more beautiful to them than any other well. They are so comfortable in their

Have you seen the face of the Divine?

well that they will very likely never search for the river. They do not know what they are missing, or even that they are missing anything at all. My student's father was present when a man who had recently been baptized was giving witness to his faith. The man was so overcome with his experience that he was brought to tears. My student's father remarked afterward that he envied this man's experience. He felt that he would be forever deprived of such an experience because, having been baptized as a baby he was not in need of conversion. Rather than sensing that his envy might be a sign of something incomplete or missing in his life, he saw his baptismal experience as over, done, in the past; he would therefore never allow himself to have the mystical experience of being initiated into the river of God's love.

The man who was giving witness was baptized in the river. My student's father was baptized in the well.

Why would we want to seek the river? Those who are baptized in the river will have an ever-deepening experience similar to the one Jesus had when the heavens opened and God's voice was heard: "You are my Son, whom I love; with you I am well pleased" (Mark 1:11). The river is the same living water that Jesus described to the Samaritan woman at Jacob's well when he said, "Everyone who drinks this water will be thirsty again, but whoever drinks the water I give him will never thirst. Indeed, the water I give him will become in him a spring of water welling up to eternal life" (John 4:13–14).

When the Lord comes, he will ask, "Did you know me?" "Have you seen the face of God?" "Have you experienced the Divine?" Did you see the river, or were you so lost in the well that it became an obstacle rather than a pathway to the river?

Once you have seen the face of God, going to church becomes meaningful, being a Christian makes sense, and all your good works will be fruitful. The well will no longer be a barrier between you and God but will open up to the river and will flow into the river, and the river into it.

4 The River of Life Is Free

Psychologist Carl Jung told us that the river of life, the river of divine love, springs forth in different places. Each time this spring is discovered, people immediately build a shrine to protect the life-giving water and make it the property of the guardians of religion. Soon there is a fee, and, of course, some groups of people are kept away from the life-giving spring. The water is not happy and so disappears from there and springs forth in another place, and another place, each time it is enshrined.

Jung believed that the spring of life-giving water now flows in what he called our shadow, that dark side of our personality that surprises us at times. Our shadow is made of the repressed aspects of our conscious self, the things the conscious person does not wish to accept within him- or herself. For instance, someone who identifies with being generous has a shadow that is stingy or selfish. Jung believed that the spring of life-giving water is more readily found in our shadow than in our limiting ego. No one thinks of building a shrine at those times when our shadow reigns, and so the waters that spring up there remain free and happy. It is here that we more easily experience the presence of the Divine. Remember, the demons always recognized who Jesus was before the religious folks of his time did. And religion can sometimes become an obstacle to experiencing the river of life and relating with the Divine.

Consider this story:

There was once a very religious man. One day he heard the voice of God in his prayer inviting him to come to a certain mountain where he would be able to see the face of the Divine and experience God's loving embrace.

The man came out of his prayer and could not contain himself. He thought of this day when he would see God face-to-face, and he just could not wait. But then he thought to himself, *I have to offer God something in return for such a wonderful gift and to commemorate this once-in-a-lifetime occasion.* He thought of gold, silver, precious stones—but nothing in the material world seemed to suffice. Finally, he decided to fill a jar with tiny pebbles. Each one of these pebbles would represent one of his prayers, sacrifices, or good works. When the jar was finally full of his little pebbles, he ran up the mountain. He got to the top, and his heart was ready to explode in anticipation. But to his surprise, he could not see or feel anything divine. He began to think that he was deluded, a victim of a divine prank. Holding his jar, he broke down and began to weep. Just then, he heard God's voice once again, saying, "I am waiting to show myself to you and wanting so much to take you into my loving arms, but you have put an obstacle between us. If you want to see my divine face and experience my love, break that jar!"

The divine gifts cannot be *earned*. If we truly believe, with Paul, that we are children of God and therefore heirs to the Divine (Romans 8:17), then the gifts of God are not our privilege but our right. They are ours to be experienced freely.

5 God—an Experience, Not a Theology

A holy man sitting atop the Himalayas put up a big sign that read, "For two cents, I will give you an experience of God." People came from all around to see him. He told them to place their money in a little bowl beside him, and then he gave them a few grains of sugar. He told them to eat the sugar. He did not ask them to describe its taste or talk about its sweetness. He had them eat the sugar and experience the sugar. What is sweetness? It can be analyzed in a chemist's laboratory. It can be described and talked about. But the more you *talk* about sweetness, the less you know what sweetness is in your mouth. Sweetness is an experience. God is an experience.

How can you prove the reality of God or the existence of God? Can you *prove* the existence of God? I like Carl Jung's definition of reality. Reality is that which affects you. Whatever affects you is real. God affects my life, so God is real for me. God motivates me, so God is real for me. God touches me; therefore, he is real for me. God opens up infinite possibilities for me, and so I am alive, and God becomes ever more real for me.

In India, there is a group of tribals who are living signs that God is an experience. They are the original inhabitants of the country. They are also the group that has been the most exploited. In the part of the country where they live, the feudal system still exists. The feudal lord owns land as far as the eye can see and owns everything on that land: the trees, the cattle, the men, the women, the children. He can do whatever he wants with whatever and whoever is on that land. He can treat all within his land with respect and reverence, but he can also beat the men, rape the women, and starve the children to death, and this is what happens—and there is no law that will prosecute him.

Each morning, these tribal people go to work in the landlord's fields, and they are happy and laughing. Their chatter can be heard across the fields, and it is free and light. At night, if the weather is good, they get their drums out and sing and dance the night away. They have very little in their homes. Their typical house is two rooms: the cattle stay in one room, and the family lives in the other. A bamboo partition separates the family from the cattle. These people have little, and yet they are happy and they celebrate life.

What gives them this freedom when they are in the midst of such pain and suffering, when their men are beaten for no reason, their women are raped, and their children are starved to death? Despite this suffering, they live fully. This does not mean that when their men are beaten, they feel no pain. They feel anger when their women are raped. When their children die, they mourn. Yet all this evil, which is part of their personal daily experience, does not stop them from living fully. When asked, "What gives you the freedom to sing and dance, to laugh, to

God is an experience.

live life so fully?" they will show you their tattoos. They are tattooed on their foreheads, their temples, their wrists, and their ankles. Each tattoo is a symbol of the Divine.

These tribals are not Catholic; they are not Christian; they are not Hindu or Buddhist. They are not part of any religion. They are nature worshippers, but they have the experience of truth, and they have the freedom that religion does not give. They believe that while they are alive, their men can be beaten, their women can be raped, their children can be starved to death, but no one can touch the Divine who is rooted in their lives. They know that when they die, friends and relatives will come and take away the few belongings that they have. Everything can be taken from them, but no one on earth can touch the Divine who is tattooed on them. All they take with them is the Divine tattooed upon them. This is their reality, their experience, and their truth.

Seeking Truth and Freedom 6

I was born in Goa, and I have lived most of my life in India. However, I earned my PhD and have spent the past fifteen summers teaching students of all ages at Saint Louis University, in the heartland of America. I can tell you with confidence that there is a difference between the Eastern and the Western understanding of truth. The Western understanding of truth is a philosophy. It is a set of beliefs that you can think about and *know*. The Eastern understanding of truth is an *experience*. It is an experience that can contradict philosophy, defy science, challenge the Scriptures and yet, in the Eastern view, be truth.

During my first semester as a theology student at St. Louis University, I was told by one of my teachers that I was a heretic and was going to hell. I had said to him, "I know that Jesus is a historical figure—I know that. But what if Scripture scholars suddenly were to tell us irrefutably that Jesus never existed, that it was all a myth, a story that had been made up?" I asked him, "What would happen to you?" My teacher, a priest who had been teaching theology for many years, replied, "If they told me irrefutably that Jesus did not exist, I would give up being a priest, being a religious, being a Christian." He said he could not base his life on a myth. Then he asked me, "What about you?" I responded that I would still die for the myth. My teacher had answered from his Western understanding of truth, and I had answered from my Eastern understanding. In the East, experience that affects life is truth. Truth is that which touches one's heart and changes one's life.

Truth in the Eastern perspective is often known and experienced in pain and suffering, whereas the truth that is experienced in comfort, luxury, and good times is sometimes an illusion. When we are confronted with pain, with suffering, with sickness and death, we know what truth is—truth becomes an experience. For some groups in India, the threat of death is a daily experience. Truth, for them, is not an idea or a philosophy. Because these people experience death every day, they fully *live* their lives. Because they are oppressed by evil, they *know* what freedom is. When we are protected from pain, we don't know what freedom is—freedom stays only an idea; it is not an experience. When our health is protected,

Truth is that which touches one's heart and changes one's life.

when we believe that we will never die, we do not know the truth of being alive. The advertisements tell us that there is always tomorrow: *You have time. Years and years.* For those groups in India, every

day is a gift, because they do not know if they will be alive tomorrow. So they live as fully as they can every day, because there might not be a tomorrow to live.

The Buddha tells a story about freedom that goes something like this: A man is walking on a road through a wooded area. Suddenly he is struck down by an arrow. The arrow lodges in his chest. He is lying bleeding beside the road when another man comes along and attempts to help him. As the second man tries to remove the arrow without hurting the first man further, the wounded man struggles to sit up and says, "Wait, wait . . . first tell me: did you see who shot the arrow? Which direction did it come from? Was the archer a Hindu, a Christian, a Buddhist, or a Muslim? Was the person male or female, rich or poor, friend or foe, progressive or conservative? Was it an accident, or was it deliberately aimed at me? What kind of punishment will the shooter receive after he dies? Do you believe in hell? And you—are you a believer? Does the arrow look like it's made of wood or of steel? Did you see anything—anything at all?" The second man says, "What I can see is that you are in pain, that you are suffering, and that you will die if we can't remove this arrow. So please stop asking useless questions and let me help you." He gives a yank on the arrow's shaft, and once it is removed the pain ceases—and so do the man's useless questions.

Freedom is an experience best understood in the living, but first you must remove the arrow of your bondage without causing yourself mortal suffering. Like the injured man in the story who is distracted from what must be done, you are distracted from living fully by the pain of your own internal arrow. Most founders of religions teach us how to live life effectively and freely in this world. Only when we begin to experience inner freedom does the path to an infinite God open up to us.

7 Can You Be Religious without Knowing God?

The Old Testament Scriptures tell a story about the boy Samuel, who spent his life in the sanctuary of the Jewish temple. Samuel was very committed to his religion. Like every religion, his was composed of a creed, a code, a cult, and a community. He knew the creed (what to believe), followed the Mosaic code (the law, how to behave), was perfect in the cult (performing the rituals and practicing the traditions), and was recognized as a potentially prominent member of the community. Yet he did not seem to have a relationship with God. When God called him, Samuel did not know him. Similarly, the high priest Eli spent all his time in the temple, and even *he* did not know God. Can a person have a religion without knowing God? Can a person know God without belonging to an organized religion?

How can a person recognize in his or her life the difference between merely practicing religion and actually developing a living relationship with God? In my experience, I have observed that those who practice religion without an active relationship with God practice *charity*, while those who have a relationship with God live a life of *compassion*. To give you a sense of what I mean by these words, I would describe myself as being engaged in charity when I am in control of the situation: I can decide who I am going to help, how long I am going to be of service, and the price I am willing to pay. Ultimately, I decide. When I am compassionate, I do not decide. I have no control—I am sucked into the situation. I am not concerned with who the person is, or what the person needs from me, or how long I am going to be with the person, or the price I will have to pay. The consequences are secondary to the call for compassionate action in the present moment.

The contrast between religion and a living relationship with God is most easily explained by some examples:

During my first graduate semester at Saint Louis University, I was invited to say a "pizza Mass." I soon discovered that this was much like the Mass I knew, except that after the Mass there was pizza for everyone. Students from different areas of the campus met in a dormitory chapel for this pizza Mass. That night we had a beautiful service—what I thought was a meaningful liturgy and a prayerful Mass. I would look up during periods of silence and see that the students were praying. There was beautiful singing and—as the students always enjoy—lots of hugging at the beginning, middle, and end.

The Mass ended, and everyone was having a good time until someone said, "Where is the pizza?" Of course, the students erupted in a chorus: "What happened to the pizza? Why isn't the pizza here?" The girl who was in charge of the pizza told us, "This guy has never let me down. Anytime I have ordered pizzas, he has always come early, and he has always delivered the pizzas." So she phoned the manager to tell him that no one had shown up with the pizzas yet.

When the girl came back to this group of students who had just prayed and celebrated the Eucharist together, she said, "I called the manager, and he said that the man who was supposed to deliver the pizzas was stabbed. He himself still has the deliveryman's blood on his clothes, and he rushed the driver to the hospital. He does not have anyone to deliver our pizzas, but if we have cars, he is ready to give them to us." What happened next shocked me. Several of the students got together to pick up the pizzas, and when they returned, the party went on as if nothing had happened. A man had been stabbed; this man might die. The man had a brother and a sister, perhaps. Certainly, he had a mother and a family. But for the students, none of this mattered. I asked myself: having just celebrated this Eucharist, do I feel connected with human suffering?

How can a person recognize in his or her life the difference between merely practicing religion and actually developing a living relationship with God?

This first story illustrates what I believe may have been an unanswered call to compassion. The following story is an instance of a person allowing herself to act with compassion when she is called to do so—literally, in this case.

Some years ago, when my mother was dying, she was in the hospital and needed blood. One of our Jesuit colleges gave my sister a list of blood-donor matches, and she got on the phone and started calling people on the list. The last call she made was answered by a Hindu woman, who said, "My son is not in town today—why do you want him?" My sister replied, "I got this list from his college, and he has the same blood type as my mother does, and my mother is in the hospital in need of blood."

The woman told my sister, "My blood type is the same as my son's. I'm coming down." She came to the hospital, and for some reason the staff could not take her blood that morning, but that Hindu woman spent the whole morning and the whole afternoon with my sister, being a mother to her. She was a stranger. She did not know our family. We did not have the same religion. We do not know her anymore. But that day she said, "My blood type is the same; I am coming down to give my blood" and spent the whole morning and the whole afternoon being a mother to my sister. That, for me, is an act of compassion, not charity.

When there is a need and the one who answers does not even take the time to think, *that* is compassion. You just move. You just respond. There is no self-consciousness. You do not pause to calculate, *Is the price I'll have to pay for being in this situation worth it?* You do not stop to reflect, *I wonder what heavenly rewards I'll get for this good deed?* You just act. Because—in a way that you are not even aware of—you are flowing with divine compassion. Perhaps you will argue that this is a matter of cultural difference, but I think I could point out to you that charity and compassion look the same no matter what side of the globe you are on.

Take this more extreme example—it is highly unrealistic, but it serves to illustrate the point without having a specific cultural context. A young man and woman have just married and are living together in an apartment. One evening, a man breaks into their home and holds the husband at gunpoint. The burglar draws a little circle around the young man and says, "If you take one step out of that circle, I will kill you." The burglar goes only a few steps away, rapes the man's wife right in front of him, and then runs out of the apartment. As soon as the burglar leaves the house, the husband is jumping up and down, happy and relieved. The wife asks, "What are you happy about? Didn't you see what that man just did? He raped me!" But her husband says, "But you don't know, my dear—when he was not looking, I put my foot out of that circle three times!"

This is charity. When people are hurting, when people are being raped, when there is so much injustice and oppression, I am jumping up and down because I have sent a check or I have given supplies to a charity. I have gone to a homeless shelter, and I have helped over the weekend. I have given my time, my money, my possessions—and I am jumping up and down because I have done something and I feel good about myself.

Now, I am not saying this is bad, so please do not get me wrong. Charity is good. Charity is wonderful. Continue doing it. Continue to do it, because it is better to do something than to do nothing in situations like this. But that list of good deeds does not count when you go up to heaven, because when Jesus says, "I was hungry and you gave me something to eat," and you say, "Yes"; when he says, "I was thirsty and you gave me something to drink," and you say, "I remember"—all of a sudden you will hear Jesus say, "I am not talking about you. I am talking about those who say, 'Lord, *when* did we see you hungry and feed you? *When* did we see you thirsty and give you something to drink? We don't remember.'" These are the people who practice compassion. If you practice compassion, you do not keep an account. You do not keep a note. You do not bring your accountant and your checkbook up to heaven. If you bring them, they will go against you.

People who have a living relationship with God are people who live by compassion. Whenever they do anything to help another human being, they wonder why people would make such a big deal about it. "Wouldn't anyone do what we just did?" is their spontaneous response. Because of their relationship with the Divine, they experience an interconnectedness with the rest of humanity and the whole of creation. What happens to one will affect the rest.

8 Moving from Charity to Compassion

In one of his stories, Joseph Campbell, the twentieth-century writer and professor of comparative religion and mythology, talks about a mountain in Bali where people from all over the world go to experience the power of the wind that comes from the valleys. It is also a place where many people go to commit suicide. Joseph Campbell tells of a man who was going to commit suicide; he was going to jump off that mountain and kill himself. Two policemen were driving through the area at the time, and the policeman who was not driving saw the man who was going to jump. That policeman opened the car door, ran to the man, and caught him just as he was falling off the mountain. The jumper was hanging over the edge, held by the policeman, and slowly began dragging the policeman to his death. The policeman could not stop the momentum slowly pulling him down. Had it not been for the policeman's partner, who came just in time, grabbed the policeman, and helped lift the two back to safety, both men would have died.

Of course, right away the media was there. TV cameras, reporters, and bystanders watched in amazement. And all were asking the policeman, "Why did you not let that man go and save yourself, save your life? You could have just let go, and you would have been safe!" The policeman replied, "If I had let that man go, I would not have been able to live another day of my life." He said that the jumper was certainly a stranger, perhaps even a criminal, or someone who was going to kill himself anyway. But that man was a part of him. "I was drawn, I was sucked into that situation. When I was holding on to that man, I was not thinking about my wife, who loves me dearly and whom I love with all my heart. I wasn't thinking of my little children, who mean everything to me, who depend on me. And least of all was I thinking about my career. All that I thought about was that if I let this man go, I will not be able to live another day of my life. If that man had died, a part of me would have died too."

Experiencing that human interconnectedness through our divine connection is the transition from charity to compassion.

That is compassion: when you are so present to life that *life chooses you*—you do not choose life. Whatever his religion, this policeman's God was a God of compassion.

Do not stop practicing your charity, but pray for the grace of being more and more compassionate. Because when you have a relationship with God, when you are compassionate, you will experience God everywhere. When you have a relationship with a compassionate God, good things happen, *wonderful* things happen. In compassion, I celebrate the good, because that good is also a part of me. When some person in the world does something extraordinary, I am drawn to that person, and I also feel extraordinary. I share in that experience because that person is part of me. If someone is celebrating, I celebrate with that person. If someone is hurting, I hurt with that person. So I am part of every person's life, and each person is part of my life. Experiencing that human interconnectedness through our divine connection is the transition from charity to compassion.

Do You Have a Living Relationship with God, or Are You Just Practicing Religion?

9

Here is a little test to determine whether you have a living relationship with God or you just practice religion: Imagine yourself as a passenger on the *Titanic*, and it is sinking. Then see yourself in a lifeboat all by yourself, safe and secure. Around your lifeboat are little children struggling to stay afloat. You can reach out to them and save them all. But a little off in the distance are your loved ones—your father, your mother, your brothers and sisters, your children perhaps, maybe your spouse or the love of your life. If you do not try to reach out to them, they will all certainly drown and die. Unfortunately, you cannot save both the children and your loved ones. Who would you save?

Now, if you save the children who are physically closest to you and painfully watch your loved ones die, you have the compassion that comes from a deep relationship with the Divine. Your God is an infinite God connecting and unifying all. Who is my father, my mother, my brothers and sisters?

Everyone is. And if you reach out to your loved ones because they have supported you and cared for you and you have a relationship with them of mutual dedication and commitment of some kind, this is good, but you practice charity that comes from religion and has the self as motivation. This act of charity is good, but we need to strive to attain the ideal of compassion.

So let us pray for the grace of being compassionate. In a living relationship with God, we are connected to and affected by what happens to *anyone* in life. With an infinitely big God, color fades away, creed fades away. Good and bad fade away. We can see beyond color, beyond religion, beyond a person being morally good or bad. As Jesus said, "I condemn the sin but never the sinner." The sinner is also me. I praise virtue, but again that person who is virtuous is also me. This is when I know I am in a living relationship with the Divine: when I can relate to another person's interior being, and I care about the world as much as I care about myself.

> *In a living relationship with God, we are connected to and affected by what happens to anyone in life.*

When I put this case to my students at the university, one of them challenged, "So in compassion you do not have any freedom!" But as I told this student, freedom comes with response plus ability. The ability to respond is freedom. In charity, my ability to respond is limited to the people I choose to help, the time I choose to give, and the price I'm willing to pay. In compassion, the ability to respond is total.

Do You Want Peace . . . without Batting an Eye?

10

O nce there was a general who was infamous for his viciousness. He was brutal, without mercy. He went to attack a small village that lay in the path of his army. Everyone in the village, knowing of the general's reputation, ran away—everyone except one man. When the general entered the village, he found this one man sitting calmly under a tree. So the general went up to the man and said, "Do you know who I am, and do you know what I'm capable of? I can run my sword right through you without batting an eye!" And the man said, "I know." Looking at the general, he continued, "But do you know who I am and what I'm capable of? I'll let you do it . . . without batting an eye."

I'll let you do it, without batting an eye. This is a beautiful story. And when we are looking at the difference between practicing religion and developing a living relationship with the Divine, it's revealing to reflect on how we respond when we are attacked and on our relationship with peace. Clearly the behavior of the general is not right. It's not good. It's not healthy. But what is our response to such behavior? What do we teach our children? What do we teach each other? Do we react with "We've got to punish this man. We've got to destroy him"? If so, if our reaction is an eye for an eye and a tooth for a tooth, then we're no better than the general. And that general—or those who behave like him—are feeding off, are soaking up our negative, destructive thoughts and behaviors.

But if my response—like the response of the man in the village, and as Jesus teaches—is one of peace, one of reconciliation, then I offer a better alternative, and that very response *does* begin to make a change. If my response is to first see this general or similarly behaving people as no less human—in fact, as divine beings—then the world begins to be a different place.

Now, I'm not suggesting that we teach our children to let themselves be slaughtered; we need to do everything we can do in a civilized world to protect the weak and vulnerable. The challenge is to determine our ultimate goal. Do we want to punish, to kill, to wipe out this person? Or do we want a resolution? Do we want peace?

If you want peace, work for peace. Respond with peace. Be peace.

It's like Jesus' teaching: if somebody strikes us on the left cheek, we offer the right cheek. And we offer it not because we're helpless, but because we are strong.

Now you might ask, Okay, but *how* do I do this? Well, to start with, if you want to change, all you have to change is a thought. Everything begins with a thought. Change your thinking, change a thought, and you will be a changed person. That thought will be expressed in your words, will affect your feelings, and will guide your behavior. And the words, feelings, and behaviors you send out into the world affect the world around you. Begin by doing it for just two minutes every day. It becomes an addiction. That is change.

If you want peace, work for peace. Respond with peace. Be peace.

Can you change just one thought? Can you know who you are in your mind, in your very consciousness, enough to think peace, act in peace, be peace . . . without batting an eye?

11 Four Ways of Relating with God

I n *The Spiritual Exercises*, St. Ignatius of Loyola's classic text, he begins by saying that we were created to praise, reverence, and serve God, our Lord. When Ignatius says praise, reverence, and serve God, our Lord, he is talking about a relationship with God. He is inviting us into union and communion with the Divine. Ignatius wants us to find any and every means to seek God and deepen our relationship with the Divine.

Who is your God? Jesus once asked his disciples this question: "Who do people say I am?" And then he confronted them: "Who do you say I am?" The disciples of Jesus had unique and very personal answers to this question: for Peter it was "Master"; for John it was "the Lord"; Thomas responded with "my Lord and my God"; and Mary Magdalene exclaimed, "Rabboni."

Jesus' question continues to echo in time, seeking a personal response from each of us who heed his call. Who is God for me? Do I have a relationship with God, or is my religion just a ritual? And if I do have a relationship with God, what kind of God do I have? A limited God or an infinite God? A God subject to human standards or a God who is ever and ever more surprising, loving, merciful, awesome, sublime?

 To help us clarify our relationship with God and understand who God is for us, let's turn to the Pentateuch, the first five books of the Bible. In the Pentateuch, there are four different experiences of God, four distinct ways of answering the question, who is God? Who is *my* God?

When Jesus walked the earth, he was not attempting to create a new religion—he wanted us to experience the Divine.

Remember that Jesus is not looking for a theology of God, but a personal experience of the Divine. When Jesus walked the earth, he was not attempting to create a new religion—he wanted us to experience the Divine. Jesus told us, "I have come that [you] may have life, and have it to the full" (John 10:10), and he prayed to God "that all of them may be one, Father, just as you are in me and I am in you" (John 17:21). The fullness of life comes from commingling with the Divine.

12 Pleasing God—the Priestly Experience

The first experience of God in the Pentateuch is in the first chapter of the book of Genesis—the first creation story. In the beginning, there was chaos, there was confusion, there was a void, there was darkness on the face of the earth. Out of that chaos and confusion, God brought forth a good and beautiful creation. On the sixth day, God said, "Let us make humans in our image, in our likeness," and he created them male and female. And God saw that what he created was very, very good. God was pleased with what he created. On the seventh day, God rested and made it holy and called that day the Sabbath.

This is the God of the priestly tradition. Let me explain:

In the experience of God found in the first chapter of Genesis, God is the Great Other and the creator of all things. There is order and a hierarchy in creation. Humans are the pinnacle of God's creation, and God shares his dominion over the whole of creation with them. The Sabbath is the axle that holds everything together in this tradition. On the Sabbath, you came to the temple, and in the temple was the priest, who mediated between you and God. People approached God through the priest, the ritual, and the temple.

In the priestly tradition, God's love must be merited by pleasing the Divine through prayer, good works, and obedience to the rituals of the church. And pleasing God is an effective way of growing in relationship with God.

How do you know if your God is a priestly God? If you believe that you need a priest to be the bridge to help you connect to God, then your God is a priestly God. If you believe that the priests and the rituals of the church guide you toward grace, then your experience of God is in the priestly tradition. If you live with fear that God will withdraw his love if you do not please him enough, then your God is a priestly God. If, when you reflect on your personal life from childhood onward, you find that you have lived to please everyone, then your God is likely a priestly God. If you believe that reverently following the creed and the traditions of your religion is what God desires of you, and that if you do so throughout your life God will bless you with entry into his heavenly kingdom, then you are relating to God in the priestly tradition. If your vision of heaven is of angels singing "Holy, Holy, Holy," of incense and candles—then your God is the priestly God, the Great Other.

13 The God of Brokenness—the Yahwistic Experience

In the second chapter of Genesis, God starts creating all over again. What happened? Did he forget that he had created the world? Was he disappointed with what he had created? No. This is an expression of another experience of God. This is another way of answering the question, who is God? It is another mode of relating to God, of seeking God.

In the second chapter of Genesis, we are told that God created man and woman out of clay. We find God not out there, not up there somewhere, but down in the clay and playing with the clay. He has his fingers, his hands, himself in that clay, and he molds that clay into the shape of a man and breathes into that clay his own breath of life. He breathes himself into that clay. That man becomes a living being, and out of that man, God creates woman. When he creates this man and this woman, he does not give them dominion over the whole of creation. He sends them as companions to work. He sends them to till the ground. He makes them co-creators. They have to complete what God has started, so they become co-creators with God.

This second experience is called Yahwistic. Yahweh is a name for God, a proper name. Yahweh talks to Adam and Eve. He walks with them in the cool of the evening. He will eat with Abraham. This God is intimate. And having breathed himself into man, he has become one with humanity. This God has become one with brokenness. What is clay? Clay stands for weakness, imperfection, and sinfulness—that which has no structure, no integrity of its own. God becomes one with broken humanity when he becomes one with the clay.

I would like to explain further what I mean when I say that God has become one with brokenness, one with clay. We see this in the story of Abraham's call (Genesis 12). God calls Abraham and tells him that he will become the father of nations. Our father in faith, Abraham, in the Yahwistic tradition, is a liar. And yet he is blessed by God and a channel of God's blessing. When Abraham goes into Egypt, Pharaoh's men ask him about the beautiful woman who is traveling with him. Although it is Abraham's wife, Sarah, he replies, "She is my sister." Why did he say that Sarah, his wife, was his sister? Because if Abraham had said that Sarah was his wife, they would have killed him and taken Sarah to Pharaoh and made her one of his concubines. Our father in faith, to save his life, tells a lie. But in the Yahwistic tradition, God continues to bless Abraham, and God blesses Pharaoh and Pharaoh's household through this liar, because the Yahwistic God never forgets that Abraham is clay, Abraham is weak, imperfect, and sinful.

Similarly, in the story of Jacob and his father-in-law, Laban (Genesis 30), we are told that Jacob was taking care of

Laban's sheep, and Jacob's sheep began to multiply. How did his sheep multiply? He *stole* them. Our great father Jacob was a thief—and yet Jacob was a channel of God's blessing. Jacob was God's chosen one, because in the Yahwistic tradition, God never forgets that Jacob is also made of clay—weakness, imperfection, sinfulness.

In the story of Jacob and Esau (Genesis 25:19–34), Esau comes home hungry, goes to his brother, Jacob, and says, "Give me something to eat, for I am dying of starvation." Jacob demands the firstborn Esau's birthright in exchange for something to eat. Poor Esau says to himself, *What is the use of my birthright if I am going to die anyway?* He says to Jacob, "Take my birthright, and give me food to eat." In the Yahwistic tradition, this man who takes advantage of his brother's situation is still God's prophet, is still blessed by God, because God never forgets that Jacob, like Abraham and all of us, is made of clay: weak, imperfect, and sinful.

How do you know if your God is a Yahwistic God? If your God is intimate with you, with humanity, then your God is the Yawistic God. If you can accept yourself in your brokenness and experience God's love in your weakness, imperfection, and sinfulness, then your God is the Yahwistic God. If you can accept others in their brokenness, then your God is the Yahwistic God. In every family, for example, there is someone who just does not turn out right. The one with a Yahwistic God will find a way to stay connected with this person. In every religious community, there will be someone who is despised by the rest—the Yahwistic person will seek out this alienated one. In many work situations, there will be a co-worker who is the topic of gossip—the Yahwistic person will befriend that person. If, however, you are content with God loving you unconditionally and you do not reach out to broken humanity, then your God may not be the Yahwistic God. But if your image of God is the father of the prodigal son, who simply says, "Finally, you have arrived!" more than likely your God is the Yahwistic God.

14 The God of Perfection—the Elohistic Experience

The third experience of God found in the first five books of the Bible is Elohistic. Elohim means "the Great God" but is not a proper name like Yahweh. You cannot see this Elohistic God face-to-face. If you do, you will die. So the Elohistic God does not walk and talk intimately with people. The Elohistic God appears in dreams. The Elohistic God appears in a cloud. The Elohistic God moves as a pillar of fire—but you cannot see this God face-to-face and live. In the Elohistic tradition, God does not become one with humanity's brokenness, because God can never be less than God, the pure Great God.

The relationship between the Elohistic God and people is one of perfection. You have to be perfect as your heavenly Father is perfect. You cannot be weak and yet be blessed by God. You cannot be sinful, insincere, or unholy and yet be God's prophet. You cannot have imperfections and expect to receive God's gifts and blessings. So what do you do? You overcome your weakness by willpower and through grace. You have to be perfect as God is perfect, pure as God is pure if you want to be blessed by God and have God enter you so that you can be God's channel, God's prophet, God's witness.

The Elohistic tradition tells some of the same stories that are told in the Yahwistic tradition—but with its own twist. In the Elohists' version of the story of Abraham going down into Egypt (Genesis 12), as in the Yahwistic version, Pharaoh's men come up to Abraham and say, "Who is this woman?" and Abraham says of his wife, "She is my sister." But the Yahwistic tradition stops there, while the Elohistic tradition continues and says that Abraham did not tell a lie. Abraham and Sarah *were* brother and sister. They had the same father but different mothers; because it was the cultural tradition of that time, such marriages were not unusual. Now, why does the Elohistic tradition want to insist on this? Because Abraham cannot willingly tell a lie and be blessed by God or be a channel of God's blessing. This tradition will also tell the story of Jacob and the sheep (Genesis 30), but it will say that Jacob's sheep multiplied not because he was stealing but because God blessed the sheep, and therefore they multiplied. Jacob cannot be a thief, cannot be weak, imperfect, and sinful and yet be a channel of God's blessing or God's witness. Elohists will tell the story of Jacob and Esau (Genesis 25), but in this tradition their mother becomes the villain. She is the one who influences Jacob to steal the birthright from his brother, Esau. Jacob cannot be weak, unjust, and sinful and yet be God's prophet.

The Elohistic tradition continues right into the New Testament. In the Gospel of Mark, we are told that one day when Jesus was walking along the road, the sons of Zebedee—the disciples James and John—went up to him and said, "Jesus, when you establish your kingdom, put one of us on your right and the other on your left. We will do great things for your kingdom." These were ambitious people, and yet they were pillars of the church; they were the apostles of Jesus. This is one Gospel version, and this account could be understood to be in the Yahwistic tradition. In the Gospel of Matthew, we are told the same story, but again there's a twist. It is not the disciples James and John who go up to Jesus, but their mother. Why this change? Because the apostles had to be perfect and holy, so the mother becomes the ambitious one. This is the Elohistic tradition, in which you have to be perfect in order to be God's witness, in order to be a channel of God's blessing, and in order to receive blessings from God.

How do you know if your God is the Elohistic God? If you are concerned about the weaknesses, imperfections, and sinfulness in your own life and devote yourself to cleansing your soul, your God is the Elohistic God. If you are distressed over the weaknesses and sinfulness of others, your God is the Elohistic God. If you see God as transcendent and unknowable to the human mind—or if you seek through God's power to transcend the human condition—then your God is the Elohistic God. If you are constantly straightening pictures, putting things at right angles, or trying to bring things into order and harmony, then your God may be the Elohistic God. When you think about life after death, if you expect servants of God to say, "You know, those imperfections of yours—you haven't really worked on them. You have to go to purgatory, get purified, and come back," you might believe in the Elohistic God.

The Pathway of the Law—the Experience of Deuteronomy

The fourth experience of God that we are shown in the Hebrew Scriptures is that of Deuteronomy. Deuteronomy is the tradition of the law. It is a simple tradition: If you keep the law, you will be rewarded. If you break the law, you will be punished. God established the law when God created the universe. The law is simply the way things are. The Deuteronomic tradition is the tradition that talks about the Last Judgment, the book of life, and the scales. How we live out eternity will be determined by the scales; it will depend on what is written in the book of life.

This fourth experience of God is expressed best in the book of Deuteronomy, which begins by exhorting the people to obey the divine decrees and warns them against abandoning the God of their fathers (1–4:40). The motivation offered is the intimate covenant that God made with the people at Mount Sinai (5–26). The book then goes on to spell out blessings on those who obey the law and curses on the rebellious. Faithfulness to the Sinai covenant would earn the people blessings not only on themselves but on their descendants (27–30).

Whenever I think about the Deuteronomy experience, I always think of Marilyn Monroe.

When Marilyn Monroe goes up to heaven, Peter opens the book of life and says, "My, my, my, Marilyn, I do not think I can take you into heaven. You have to go to hell. You have lived such a riotous life that heaven is not the place for you." Marilyn Monroe says, "Peter, all that you have written is true, but my heart is pure, my heart is clean." Peter continues to insist that she go to hell, and Marilyn Monroe continues to insist all the more that she was good and deserves to go to heaven.

So Peter goes to Jesus, and Jesus says, "Oh, give her the simple test." Peter comes back and tells Marilyn Monroe, "Well, Marilyn, this is a test to see if what you are saying is true or not true. Heaven is across on the other side, and down is hell. You must walk across this rope to get to heaven, but if you have one sexual thought, you will go straight down to hell. Are you ready to do this?" Marilyn Monroe says, "Sure, Peter, my heart is clean, my heart is pure." So Marilyn Monroe starts walking, and Peter is walking behind her with the book of life. Three-fourths of the way there, Marilyn turns around. There is no Peter! Where did Peter go? Keep the law, and you will be rewarded. Break the law, and you will be punished.

So how do you know if your God is the God of Deuteronomy? If you are counting how many sins you have committed, how many virtues you have, the number of good things you have done, and the number of bad things you have done because everything in this universe balances out, then your God is the God of Deuteronomy. If you believe that creation is the way it is because God set the foundations of the universe, and that no one or nothing or no discovery is going to change how things are, then you may have a God of Deuteronomy. If you believe that there is a code to be followed, a how-to for life, then your experience of God follows the Deuteronomic tradition. When you are at the point of death, if you expect a particular judgment based on the book of life when you stand before heaven, then your God is the God of Deuteronomy.

16 Disposable Images of God

In the Indian tradition, there are 330 million gods. No one believes that any one of these gods is divine. They are expressions of human experiences of the Divine, images that point to deeper aspects of the Divine. Spiritual growth happens when one is constantly experiencing and transcending these images until one reaches the Divine with no images. Beyond images, beyond manifestations, beyond mediators, one experiences the Divine as divine.

In a similar fashion, the Christian mystics tell us—and I've come to understand through personal experience—that if we want to get deeper into the river of divine life, if we want to know an infinitely big God, then we too will have to transcend the images of God that we might have. The Divine is so great, so wondrous, so unfathomable that any image or metaphor we hang on God is at best only a partial fit and quickly limits our ability to experience other aspects.

So let's reflect for a moment on our lives and ask ourselves, Who is God for me? How have I been experiencing God? Is my God the priestly God, whom I try to please through the rituals and traditions of my faith, the Mass, my prayer, sacrifices, the church, or the temple? Is my God the Yahwistic God, with whom I feel broken, weak, imperfect, sinful, and yet loved? Is my God the Elohistic God, for whom I try to make myself perfect as my heavenly Father is perfect? Or is my God the God of Deuteronomy, for whom I focus on observing God's law, doing good deeds, and keeping track of the balance of my account in heaven?

If we want to get deeper into the river of divine life, if we want to know an infinitely big God, then we too will have to transcend the images of God that we might have.

It is important to know that each one of these traditions is a *good* tradition. Each one has produced saints. Sometimes we need priests or the temple as an intercessor to help us connect to the Divine or guide us toward grace. Sometimes we need to experience God in our brokenness, in our weakness—and other times we need to see God as so holy, ultimate, and pure that if only we were to remove our sin, God would elevate us beyond our human condition. And at times, we need to accept that what we do to others we ultimately do to ourselves, that we reap what we sow, because this is God's interconnected universe, and God doesn't play favorites.

Whatever way you relate with God, it is good; it is right. Once you recognize your way of relating with God, find ways of deepening this relationship and of integrating the best of all four traditions. By doing so, you will begin to transcend the traditions and move deeper into the river of divine intimacy. One way to start is by asking, who was the God who was introduced to me as a child? How and when did my God change? Who is God for me now, and what is a deeper expression of my relationship with the Divine?

Transcending Your Images of God

17

When I was a child, I was introduced to a God who was a monster. It took me many, many years to get rid of this monster, to destroy this image of God and transcend it so that I would have an insight—a little peek—into the living God, the true God, the God of Jesus Christ. I can summarize my childhood experience by telling you a story that I was told as a child:

A little boy had a mother who loved him very much. One day, this little boy got angry with his mother and kicked her. The mother, being so loving and good, forgave the boy. The little boy grew up to be a young man who went to college and got married. He had a family, became an old man, and then died. Everybody was there for his funeral. When the priest finished all the prayers, he went to close the coffin so they could bury the man—but the leg of the corpse suddenly sprang straight up. The people had to saw off the leg so they could close the coffin and bury the old man, who as a child had kicked his mother.

Perhaps the ones who told me this story wanted me to respect my elders: they were saying, in effect, Do not kick your mother. What did *I* hear as a young child? I heard that the man above never forgets. I was a normal child; I had imperfections and weaknesses, yet I was also good. But, as Scripture says, the just man falls seven times a day. So here I was, with my sinfulness, imperfections, and weaknesses, believing that I had no chance with God. I was going to be punished. When I had visions of my own funeral as I was growing up, I could just see the people cutting and cutting and cutting off all kinds of pieces of me so they could close the coffin and put me into the ground. So I tried to do good deeds to balance out the bad things that I did in life. The God who was introduced to me as a child was the God of Deuteronomy, the God of law.

In truth, I was frightened of the God I worshipped. I was terrified of this God because I knew I had no chance with him. This was a God who was just waiting for me to come up to heaven so he could send me to hell. That was the way I related with God. That was my experience of God—as a monster—and I was afraid to tell anybody about the way I felt.

The church of my childhood also believed we had no chance with God, so it gave us a scapular of our Lady and assured us that if we died while wearing it, Mary would smuggle us into heaven. That scapular is one of the reasons I never learned how to swim. I would go into the sea holding on to that scapular around my neck and try to swim—the best way to drown. I thought, *Just in case I go down, I want to make sure that I have the scapular around my neck, so I can go straight to heaven.* I wore the scapular morning, noon, and night until the age of seventeen, when I joined the Jesuit novitiate, where I found that they did not wear scapulars. They did not have a scapular to give me when this one wore out! One day, in fear and trembling, I took the scapular out and—in a moment of both great faith and great anxiety—burned it. That night, I stayed awake to make sure I did not die, for I knew that if I did, hell would swallow me up.

I rid myself of the fear the scapular gave me, but the church never gives up. I was also told that if I said three Hail Marys to our Lady every night, she would take me up to heaven. She would help me pass through the Judgment. My relationship with God was full of guilt and fear, and as I grew up, religion for me was not healthy or good. If someone in my family got sick, if something went wrong, I knew it was because I had done something bad; I had sinned, and the priestly God was now punishing me to show me my sinfulness. The God I believed in was a punishing God.

My experience of God began to change when I was in the eighth grade and my family moved from a Catholic ghetto into an Indian environment. For the first time, I was thrown into the Hindu world. Hinduism is full of life and fun. The festivals are packed with noise, singing, music, color, and dancing. A Bollywood movie is not so far from the truth. So in my new surroundings, I looked at my Hindu neighbors and saw a different way of experiencing God, a different way of expressing my relationship with God. This way of relating with God was not from the tradition of Deuteronomy, the tradition I knew so well. But I was told that if I approved of these Hindus, if I participated in their religious functions, then I would be committing a mortal sin and would go to hell. There's that image of a punishing God again.

Fortunately for me, my mother's gift for universal hospitality and friendship helped show me how to move beyond this image. Before some of the Hindu festivals and great celebrations of their gods, the Hindus do a sort of novena: for nine days, they dance and sing praises of God. I do not know where my Catholic mother got the courage, but she and my sisters befriended and became part of the group of women who sang and danced before the festivals.

My mother's philosophy included a belief in the infinite possibilities of life, and this allowed her to open herself to a multitude of ways of celebrating the Divine, comparable to the many Hindu celebrations of the Divine. This helped our family and our Hindu neighbors feel at home with each other. My father, on the other hand, had the gift of questioning everything, even though he too was a traditional Catholic. The answers were not important as long as he kept searching for the deeper and more relevant realities of life, especially in his ever-growing relationship with the Divine. My mother's gift of striving after infinite possibilities and my father's gift of questioning have helped me tremendously in my own life and in my journey into a deeper and deeper relationship with the Divine. These two gifts are powerful tools that serve anyone who is seeking to transcend his or her images of God.

It took me a long time to become aware that my image of God was a monster and that this monster was a small and petty God. It took even longer before I was able to fully give up this monster and open myself to a bigger God—the God who is

It took even longer before I was able to open myself to a bigger God—the God who is celebration, the God who is life, the God who is love.

celebration, the God who is life, the God who is love. When I was introduced to the four traditions of God, I began to think that maybe I would like to have the Yahwistic God as my God. I changed, slowly.

18 Can You Have a God beyond Names?

I met a Hindu girl while I was doing my teacher's training in Bombay, India, who was the first person to challenge me and inspire me to think about how big my God could be. At that time, I was one of very few Christians at the college. Most of the students and faculty were Hindus or Muslims. From day one, everyone knew I was a Jesuit priest, and they would ask me questions like "Why did you become a priest?" "Why do you not get married?" "Who is God?" "How do you pray?" "What is Christianity?" And so I thought, *This is my mission—to enlighten all these pagans.* I would take every opportunity to talk to them about the beauties of Christianity and perhaps the well of Christianity.

One day, I was telling the students about God being Father, God being Abba, God being like my daddy, and all of them were just taken up with this wonderful concept, except one girl. She was a Hindu Brahmin girl. After class, she took me aside and said, "You are a priest, and you are going to teach people about God. You know nothing about God. Your experience of God is childish—not childlike, but *childish*." She told me, "In Hinduism, we also call God *Father*, we also call

God *Daddy*; we give God about 330 million different names. Daddy, Abba, is one of those. But this is for people who cannot understand who God is. This is for little children and illiterate people and those who cannot seek God or appreciate who God is. But if you are a priest and if you are going to teach about God, you have to grow in your relationship with God. God is beyond names. God is tremendous, God is awe-inspiring, God is personal. God is very close to me, but he is also the big thing out there, the transcendent God, the omnipotent God, the tremendous God, the mysterious God." This Hindu girl put me on the path of mysticism. This Hindu girl invited me and challenged me to go beyond my religious upbringing and my understanding of God as Father and opened the door for me to have a much bigger God. In his writings, Paul constantly exhorts us to stop thinking like children and to become adults in our relation with God (see 1 Corinthians 14:20).

Thomas Aquinas teaches that God is known by what God is not. The Hindus express this same truth by the Sanskrit *Neti neti*—Not this, not that. God is Father and God is not Father. God is Mother and God is not Mother. God is divine. God is the one who reveals himself to Moses in the third chapter of the book of Exodus. Moses asks God, "What is your name?" and God answers, "I AM. I AM."

God *is*.

There is no name for God. As soon as you call God by a name, you limit God, you restrict God. You need to go beyond that name. Of course, God is Father. I—like most human beings—have a need at times to talk about God in familiar terms. But as soon as I say "Father," I know that I am limiting God. And so I try to go beyond that experience of God. That Hindu girl helped me surpass the four traditional ways of relating with God, go beyond God as Father, and encounter God on the mystical level—where God is Divine, God-who-is.

Other religious faiths share this understanding. Many years ago, I made a Buddhist retreat. The Buddhists—through their ten days of perfect silence, one meal a day, and fourteen hours a day of prayer and meditation—offer an experience of the Divine that is all-encompassing. The Divine is everywhere; you are in the Divine, and the Divine is in you. The Divine is in everything, and everything is in the Divine. Through my Buddhist experience, that tremendous, transcendent God became imminent, became personal, became everything to me. After that retreat, I was ready to encounter the Divine in daily life in a deeper and more personal way. The retreat helped me better understand my Catholic faith and my chosen pathway of Ignatian spirituality, and it fueled in me a desire for an experience of God like that of St. Ignatius, a mystical experience of unity with the Trinity that ultimately led him into the very being and essence of the Divine.

"God is beyond names. God is tremendous, God is awe-inspiring, God is personal. God is very close to me, but he is also the big thing out there, the transcendent God, the omnipotent God, the tremendous God, the mysterious God."

Desiring a God so big that names fall away, and so transcendent that God becomes personal and all and everything, can give us the freedom and the readiness to go deeper into our relationship with the Divine. Like St. Ignatius, we are drawn into the river and on into the very being and essence of God.

19 The God Who Is a Projection of Our Father Image

I once led a retreat for a Jesuit who told me that in his family there was a tradition of not saying long prayers. "Long prayers spell trouble," he said. This was difficult for me to understand until he began to talk about his father. This Jesuit's father was in the Indian army. For nine months of the year, the father would be on the front line, protecting the country against the enemy. When the father came home for his annual leave, he brought the army with him. He ruled the house as if it were the military. In addition, to ease the tension of nine months on the front line, the father would drink and sometimes get drunk and become abusive. The whole family would wait for the father to get back to taking care of the country so that they could have peace at home.

Now, when this Jesuit goes to pray, he encounters a God who is a military commander. A military God tells you everything you do wrong and can get abusive if you stay too long in his presence. It's not surprising that the time this Jesuit spends in prayer talking with God is short. He learned this from his family; their devotion to this God is short and sweet, and then they think, *Now let God leave and take care of the rest of the world, so that our lives are more peaceful and free.* This Jesuit admits that he has problems with authority. He can turn the kindest, gentlest person in authority into a military commander. On the other hand, thanks to his relationship with his mother, he has developed a deep devotion to Mary and has a wonderful way of relating with women.

The psychologist Sigmund Freud believed that God is a projection of our father image. The way we experienced our fathers in the first six years of our lives influences the way we relate with God. Today it's commonly agreed that the family environment is where fundamental values are first formed and where children are taught what it means to be a parent. And even though some would like to call God *Mother*, in the Christian collective unconscious, God is Father. So our father becomes an image of our Father.

Here's a story of two sisters I know and how their differing experiences of their father while growing up have influenced the way they relate to God.

These sisters grew up in a good Catholic home, and when they were young adults, both entered religious life— one sister joined a convent of cloistered Carmelites, and the other became active in an apostolic outreach community. The cloistered sister is a friend of mine, and one day she called me and asked me to help her pray. My first reaction was to ask her to consider leaving the convent, because I believed that the charism of the cloistered sisters was to pray, and here she was telling me that she believed she could not pray. I meant it lightheartedly, of course. In contrast, this woman's sister, who was in the apostolic community, had absolutely no difficulty in praying. I once spiritually directed her in an annual retreat; she could sit for hours on end like a Mona Lisa and pray.

Some time later, my cloistered friend began to share with me her childhood stories. She told me how, at the end of every school year, the mailman would deliver the report cards, and every child in the home would rush to open his or her report card, except the one sister who later in life could pray. She would take her envelope and place it on the altar and wait for her father to come home in the evening. After her father had checked the grades of the other kids, who reported 70 percent, 80 percent, and 90 percent marks at school, he would take the one who had not opened her envelope to the altar, say a little prayer, open the envelope . . . and then hug her and kiss her. She managed only 40 percent—just enough to pass her to the next grade.

In her relationship with God, the sister who received 40 percent marks experiences the hugs and kisses of "God her Father," while the sister who is in the cloister—the one who received the 90 percent mark—hears God say, "Good! Excellent! Keep it up!" but does not experience the warmth and affection of God her Father. She also believes that if she does not deliver her 90 percent, she may not even hear "Good, excellent, keep it up." In the first sister's apostolic outreach community, everyone is happy with her—she is given all kinds of responsibilities in India and is often sent to represent the congregation at international meetings. If you go to the cloister where the second sister lives, you will be told that she is a very gifted and talented sister, but she has never been made prioress of the convent.

Freud's notion of father-God projections does give us a helpful insight when we're deeply examining our relationship with God. If in our childhood our father was away, working hard so that the family would have a comfortable life, or if our father left the family or died, then our image of God will likely be of an absent or distant God. My own father took great delight in giving his children experiences that were unusual and unexpected. My God, therefore, was a God of surprises. This image of God constantly battled with the image that the church of my childhood instilled in me. Now, as an adult, I may understand my father better or differently, but the way I experienced him in the first six years of my life has and will continue to have an influence on my relationship with God. With this understanding, I can clarify my relationship with God, free myself from limiting images and projections, and make room for an infinite God of endless possibilities.

20 Prayer, a Pathway to Freedom and Love

The last exercise that St. Ignatius offers in *The Spiritual Exercises* is called the Contemplation to Attain Love. This is a tremendous exercise, and for centuries it has helped generations of people, on all continents, of all cultures. In this exercise, the retreatant is given four steps of prayer, of deepening one's relationship with God and one's direct experience of divine communion and personal freedom.

The first step in this exercise is to recall the gifts of your life: your birth, baptism, family, children, redemption, grace, qualities, and talents—anything and everything you have to be grateful for. In gratitude for these gifts that God has given you—and that include the Divine himself—you offer it all, including yourself, back to God.

The second step is to ponder that the Divine is in every creature by its essence, power, and presence, and especially in *you*, the temple of the Holy Spirit, made in the likeness and image of the Divine. You are the temple of God's spirit. Scripture says it clearly: God dwells in you. You are God's image and divine likeness. Here are the words of St. Ignatius: See God present in you just as God is present in a temple. See yourself as God's own image and divine likeness.

In the third step of the exercise, St. Ignatius has you think through all these gifts again and see God laboring in them. See God, like a woman in labor, working in each one of his gifts to you, and especially in you. What is a woman in labor doing? She is working to bring something to life, to bring something to fruition, to give birth in fullness, to convey life. What is God laboring to do? He is trying to perfect us, the temple where he dwells. He is trying to perfect his own image, his own likeness. He is trying to convey to us the fullness of life and make us good and beautiful. God is trying to help us see ourselves the way *he* sees us already.

The fourth step of the exercise will shatter you. To the Western mind, it will be almost impossible to accept or even believe. St. Ignatius says that *the gift becomes divine.* You and God become one, like the rays of the sun and the sun. You can distinguish the rays from the sun, but there are no rays without the sun. And there is no sun without rays. The two of them have one identity. And just in case you did not get that symbol, Ignatius goes on to say that it is like the waters of the fountain and the fountain. There is no fountain without water, and the water has its identity only in being part of the fountain.

Thus, at the end of the Spiritual Exercises, you and the Divine become one. Not only do you and God become one, but also everything is seen as a manifestation of the Divine. You look at a tree and see God and experience God. It is a manifestation of the Divine. It is the presence of the Divine that makes a tree a tree. It is a miracle.

From the energy of a tiny seed you get such a huge tree. If that is not a miracle, what is? You and I are miracles, walking miracles. Every human creature is a miracle. That is why the

God brings everything God has and pours it into the relationship, and you bring everything you have and pour it into the relationship, until you commingle, and you become one with the Divine.

poet Gerard Manley Hopkins says that "the world is charged with the grandeur of God." Everything is charged with God. Everything commands reverence.

This is the peak experience of the Spiritual Exercises—when you experience your identity in the Divine. That is the invitation of the Contemplation to Attain Love. It is an exchange between you and the Divine. God brings everything God has and pours it into the relationship, and you bring everything you have and pour it into the relationship, until you commingle, and you become one with the Divine. Your experience of the Divine in everything deepens, and you remain in contemplation, a prayerful state of being, even in the midst of living life.

Having a Honeymoon with God

For me, the point of a honeymoon is to take in a tremendous profession of love. When a couple gets married, the man and the woman come to the altar, and the man tells his wife-to-be, "I will love you in good times and in bad times, in health and in sickness. I will love you totally and unconditionally." The woman thinks, *Oh my God, this is tremendous. Let's go someplace so that we can take it in.* And she responds to the man in the same way: "I will love you totally, as God loves you, without any condition." And the man thinks, *This is fantastic. I want to celebrate and revel in this; let's spend some time letting it soak into our very being.* The man and the woman go on a honeymoon to revel in this love that they have for each other, to take in the mystery and the beauty of their spouse. This is why when people who have returned from their honeymoon talk about what they ate and what they bought, I think that maybe they did not have a real honeymoon.

When Jesus went into the desert after his baptism experience, he was doing much the same thing; he was on a honeymoon with God. Jesus' baptism, as told in the Gospels, was a tremendous experience of God. The heavens opened, the Spirit descended, and God's voice was heard: "My beloved, I am pleased with you, my favor rests on you, my delight is in you." I like to see this baptismal experience as the beginning of a new relationship with God; Jesus was discovering God in an amazing new way. This was such a wonderful experience that Jesus needed time to assimilate it, to make it a part of him, and therefore he went into the desert for forty days and forty nights.

The Catholic Church's forty days of Lent are a commemoration of the forty days that Jesus spent in the desert. During Lent, with Jesus, I have forty days to deepen my relationship with God and get deeper into the divine river. I have an opportunity to have a honeymoon with God.

This honeymoon, however, is not without its difficult moments. Although we are experiencing the Divine in fresh and deeper ways, we still face obstacles in our journey to the river. When Jesus went into the desert for his honeymoon with God, he was relishing and rejoicing in his relationship with his Father. But he also faced three temptations, and the temptations that he went through are the same stumbling blocks that every one of us encounters on our journey toward the Divine.

The first temptation we face involves the material things we desire. When Jesus went into the desert, Satan came and said, "Change this stone into bread and eat." Now, what is bread? Bread represents the material things of this world and the comforts of life. Are they good? They are very good. But Jesus said, "I have had such a wonderful experience of God that these pleasures and material things don't count at all. They are good, they are wonderful, but they are nothing compared to this tremendous experience I have had, this union and communion I have with the Father. These material things cannot be the source of my happiness and the meaning of my life." Desire for material things could not interfere with Jesus' honeymoon with God.

Jesus said to Satan that a person does not live on bread alone, but we can become overly concerned with the material things we have and want. When we are consumed with desire for these things, when we make them the source of our happiness and the goal of our life, we are drawn away from a full and deep relationship with the Divine. We accept the bread although what we need is the nourishment that only God can provide.

The second temptation we face concerns what people say and think about us. Satan took Jesus to the pinnacle of the Jewish temple and said, "Throw yourself down, and as Scripture says, 'At God's command, the angels will support you.'" What is implied here is that everybody would proclaim Jesus as Son of God, Messiah, King of kings, and Savior. Everyone would see how holy Jesus must be and say good things about him. Satan says, in essence, *Throw yourself down from your values, your truths, your relationship with God, just so that other people will know and proclaim what a great person you are.*

Jesus had the same temptation when he was hanging on the cross. The scribes and the Pharisees came and said, "If you are the Son of God, come down from the cross, and we will believe you. Throw yourself down, and we will believe you." That is our human temptation too. How often do I not fully live by the values that come from my relationship with God, just so that my children will say good things about me?

How often in my life do I compromise the values that are most precious to me in my relationship with God because I want to keep my relationship with my boyfriend, girlfriend, or spouse? How often do I keep my mouth shut in church so I can protect the good opinion that people in my parish have of me, when I think and feel differently because of my relationship with God? How often do I remain silent in the face of injustice, when my relationship with God demands otherwise?

In refusing this temptation, Jesus shows us that what people say does not matter. The people who shout, "Hosanna!" today will be the very same people who shout, "Crucify him!" tomorrow. The only thing that matters is what God says to me and what God feels toward me: I am pleased with you, my favor rests on you, my delight is in you. What matters is not if people say good or bad things about me; what matters is the way I feel in my relationship with God and that I am free. As with the pleasures of life, the good opinion of people is a good thing; to be considered honorable, moral, just, and kind is a good thing. But I cannot build my happiness around, or find meaning for my life in, what people say and think about me.

The third temptation, which most of us succumb to, is the temptation to be someone important, to have some kind of authority and power. In the desert, Satan tempted Jesus a third time by showing him the kingdoms of the world in their magnificence and saying, "All these kingdoms I will give you, if you will bow down and worship me." Jesus responded, "I am not interested in being someone in authority and power. I do not desire to rule over things or people. What is important is that my authority comes from God's love for me and my relationship with the Divine. I will not separate myself from God for the sake of power, a title, or a position."

How often in life we value people for the power they exercise or the titles they possess. How often in life we value ourselves for having these things. Think about the man who was asked what kind of a job he had and replied, "I have two hundred people under me." He was mowing the grass in the cemetery! People all too often feel their life is worthwhile in proportion to the power they have over others or how high they've reached on the totem pole. It is true that when we have a position of authority, we can do a lot of good in this world. But that position or role cannot be the source of our happiness or provide meaning for our lives. Basing happiness on positions, titles, roles in this world—or on anything less than the ultimate, less than the Divine—only leads to disappointment. Sooner or later you lose that earthly power and authority; it changes or is just taken away from you. The only power and authority that lasts is that which you cannot earn or "claim," that which comes freely from being who you are in God.

The only thing that matters is what God says to me and what God feels toward me: I am pleased with you, my favor rests on you, my delight is in you.

Jesus' baptism and desert experiences became the foundation for the rest of his life and sustained him through the ups and downs, all the way through his passion and death. In our journey toward the Divine, we face the same temptations he faced. Yes, the material things of this world are created by

God and are good; yes, people's good opinion of me is positive and good; yes, having responsibility and being a leader is to be highly regarded. But none of these are ends in themselves, nor are they absolutely necessary to our relationship with God. If they become ends in themselves, they become a block between us and our journey to the river. Like Jesus, we can honeymoon with God when we let go of all these temptations and embrace radical freedom to experience the Divine.

You Are Mine   **22**

I n Isaiah 49:15–16, the Lord says:

> Can a mother forget the baby at her breast
>> and have no compassion on the child she has borne?
> Though she may forget,
>> I will not forget you!
> See, I have engraved you on the palms of my hands.

I remember asking my Scripture professor when I was in graduate studies, "Does this mean that God has tattooed us on his body: 'I will not forget you, for I have engraved you on the palms of my hands'?" My professor told me, "Oh no, Paul, this cannot possibly mean that, because the Jews were against tattooing. But I will look into it and let you know." He was a specialist in rabbinic studies who taught the Old Testament. When he came back to class the next time, he said, "Paul, you're right: the rabbi I consulted said 'engraved on the palms of my hands' means tattooed." I was ecstatic about this, not because I wanted to be right, but because this completely validated my personal relationship with and experience of God.

My experience of God can be summed up in three words: *You are mine.*

This understanding continues to define my reality with the Divine. God is tattooed upon my body, and I am tattooed on God. The Divine and I are one. I belong to the Divine, and nothing can take that away from me. The Divine belongs to me, and nothing can take that away from God.

This understanding comes from Isaiah 43:1–7, where God says, "I have summoned you by name; you are mine." These are not just beautiful words. This is what I live by. From my childhood, even though my God at one time seemed to be a monster, one thing kept me with God: a sense of belonging. Not an intellectual sense of belonging, but a felt sense of intimacy. When I was growing up, I felt that I was a pampered and spoiled child of God. I knew that I was special to God, and I grew up believing that. On my ordination card were those same three words: *You are mine.* This was my expression of my relationship with God, and it continues to help me live my life and faith as fully as I can. I come back to this expression when I need to go to the depths of life—to celebrate life, or to understand life, or to hold life in mystery, or to confront evil. These three words have helped me live through evil, through pain, through suffering. I have been through much in my years, and I have grown because God has promised me that I am his.

Living in relationship with a big God—belonging to a big God—does not mean living without pain, without hardship. It means that every pain gives a new insight into the mystery of life, a new reason to live; every pain brings us closer to our spiritual core and gives us a new way to celebrate life.

Through all the painful experiences of my life, "You are mine" has helped me become a freer and happier person. I embrace life with much more ease, and I celebrate the joys and the beauty of life much more. Is

My experience of God can be summed up in three words: **You are mine.**

my life more painful? Perhaps. But I am freer, and I use every painful experience to come closer to experiencing the fullness of life. "You are mine" helps me understand and experience the ultimate meaning of my life. It helps me hold on to what is everlasting and real and let go of what is transient. It helps me maintain serenity of mind and heart even in the most painful and devastating situations.

"You are mine" is not an idea of the mind; it is not a concept. It is an experience of the heart, and I live by that experience—by that "truth," in the Eastern understanding of the word. That experience draws me into greater intimacy and greater love. That experience draws me into the depths of the mystery of God and into the mystery of life. And the deeper I go into this mystery, the freer and the happier I am in the midst of all my experiences, good or bad.

"You are mine" gives me the authority to proclaim the things that I am proclaiming and to live the life that I am living. "You are mine" is expressed as the meaning and the message of my life. It gives me a reason to live and a reason to die.

In your relationship with the Divine, have you experienced a God who has engraved you on his palms? Have you experienced a God who has called you by name?

23 Freedom in the Midst of Suffering

Anyone who goes through St. Ignatius's Spiritual Exercises begins with the exercise on sin. I, the retreatant, through examination and reflection, try to uncover my relationship with God. In that context, I discover myself. I discover who God is, and in that discovery, I experience who I am.

And who am I? I am the image and likeness of the Divine, created good and beautiful. Who am I? I am the one who hears God's voice, loud and clear, saying from the heavens, "My beloved, I am pleased with you. My favor rests on you. My delight is in you." That is who I am—important, precious, and beautiful. I discover myself, my true identity, in my relationship with God.

After I have found my identity, St. Ignatius continues the exercise by having me reflect on the Gospel and enter into the life and person of Jesus, who is Emmanuel. Emmanuel means "God with us." Jesus, the Divine, becomes human so that the human becomes divine. It is at this point that Ignatius introduces contemplation as a form of prayer. In Ignatian contemplation, we allow the divine mystery, the incarnate Son, to fill us and transform us into him. We watch Emmanuel like a sunflower following the sun and get soaked in the mystery of his person. When Ignatius comes to the story of the Passion, I become assimilated into the mystery. The heart and the spirit of Emmanuel become mine as I go through the painful passion and death that Emmanuel goes through.

It is here that I encounter freedom of spirit in the midst of the most excruciating pain: physical, emotional, psychological, and spiritual. I come out of the exercise on the Passion like that tribe whose people are tattooed with the Divine, and with them I can say, "You can take away all my material goods. I can still sing and dance. You can still hear the sound of my laughter. You can beat me, you can be unjust to me, you can take away all my rights, and I still will be free."

Having gone through the Ignatian Exercises many times, I find that the passion and the cross of Jesus mean two things. First, they are a consequence of living my relationship with God. A consequence of my life with God is essentially a dying, a giving up, and a self-emptying. If I have been listening to what Jesus says and following Jesus' teaching, I will be like him. I oftentimes resist being like him, because to be like him is to go through the Passion. To be like him is to be at Calvary in order to experience resurrection.

The second meaning of the Passion is Good News in action. The Good News that Jesus came to give us is freedom—not freedom from suffering, sickness, and death, but freedom that we experience *in* suffering, *in* sickness, and *in* the face of death. Jesus never promised to get rid of suffering. He never promised to get rid of sickness. He never promised to get rid of death and dying. Jesus promised to give us the peace that the world cannot give. Jesus promised to give us the inner freedom, joy, and happiness that no one and nothing can take away from us, even in the midst of tremendous pain, suffering, sickness, and death. That is the Good News of Jesus, and that is what we see in the cross. That is what we see in the Passion. That is what the mystics found when they read the Passion and prayed the Passion. The Passion was the favorite prayer of most mystics. They loved the Passion. They enjoyed the Passion. They prayed the Passion over and over and over again.

Jesus promised to give us the inner freedom, joy, and happiness that no one and nothing can take away from us, even in the midst of tremendous pain, suffering, sickness, and death.

When you read the Passion according to John, beginning with the washing of the disciples' feet in chapter 13, try to capture the heart and the spirit of Jesus. If you do, like the mystics, you will be transformed. Jesus will give you strength, and you will find meaning in the suffering and pain of your life. You will find meaning that allows you to live through difficult times. The Passion is powerful. The Passion is an invitation to empty self to be a part of the divine self. If Jesus had not washed Peter's feet, he would not have a part in the divine self.

Can You Experience the Freedom That Is Christ's Cross?

24

There was a Jesuit in Bombay who would travel from one end of the city to the other on his motorbike. One day he was in an accident, and his leg was smashed to bits. He was taken to the hospital and was cared for in the emergency room by a non-Christian doctor. When the pain would become unbearable, the Jesuit would turn toward the wall and grab the little wooden cross that he wore around his neck, then turn back and smile. The doctor treated him for about a month, trying to save his leg. One night, the doctor came to him and said, "Father, we have done everything we can. I am sorry to say we will have to amputate your leg." The Jesuit said, "That's fine," then fell into a peaceful sleep. This man who had led an active life and was now going to lose his leg had said, "Amputate my leg; I'm okay."

The doctor and the man became good friends. One day the non-Christian doctor asked the Jesuit, "Father, what is in you that gives you this freedom? When I saw you in the emergency room, I looked at you and said you were either a saint or the son of the devil himself. I have seen people less hurt and in less pain, and they would be screaming, yelling, shouting, cursing God—but you were so peaceful. That night when I came to you and tried to break the news to you about your leg being amputated, with ease you simply said, 'Go ahead,' and you went to sleep." The Jesuit brightened and replied, "Well, doctor, I know that with my leg or without my leg, God loves me all the same." And the fool, this Jesuit, believed it! You and I also say, *With my leg or without my leg, God loves me all the same*—but we add, *but don't cut off my leg!* This Jesuit was flowing with life because he believed that God loved him all the same. His belief in God's love for him was the meaning and purpose of his life. He could lose all else as long as he had God's love.

That is what we see in the cross of Jesus Christ. The cross will not save your leg. The cross will not spare you from surgery. The cross will not stop you from becoming a cripple. But the cross of Jesus Christ will give you that inner freedom to be able to say, "With my leg or without my leg, God loves me all the same. So cut it off if you have to. I can go to sleep in peace." Can you accept this freedom? Are you willing to live in God's unconditional love for you?

Here's another example of someone who embraced the liberation that Jesus proclaimed and who understood Christ's cross as Good News in action. This story is about my godmother, who lived in San Francisco.

A year before my ordination, my godmother wrote my mother that she had cancer. My mother, of course, began to cry, because we loved this woman. She was our favorite aunt. For us in India at that time, cancer was another word for death. In the next letter my godmother wrote, she said, "I am planning to come home for Christmas." My mother began to cry again, because, as she said, it would be the last time, and we would probably be welcoming a corpse into the house. My godmother arrived with her daughter, who was nine or ten. Not for one moment did any of us feel that my godmother had cancer. She was full of life. She wanted to go visit relatives. She wanted to go see places. She wanted to go shopping. She was fully alive, and yet she was condemned to die. She was going to die soon, and still she was bubbling with life.

One day my godmother sat me down and told me, "When I was first told that I had cancer and that I had a short time to live, I went into a depression. I was scared. Some friends of mine came around and said, 'Would you like to join our prayer group?' And so I went, and in that prayer group, I had a deep experience of God. I found my relationship with God. Today I do not pray for a cure for myself. I pray that God will help someone find a cure for cancer so that the thousands who come after me will profit and benefit from that cure. But there is one thing I pray for myself: that I may live one day at a time and live as fully as I can." And she did. Therefore, when she came home to India, she was full of life. She was so fully present to life that she enjoyed every moment of her stay and every moment of the rest of her life. Before she left, she told me, "I am coming back for your ordination," which would take place the following year. When she returned to San Francisco, she went back to work and continued to live one day at a time, as fully as she could.

One day she realized her time to die had come. She called her husband and said, "Please take me to the hospital." The poor husband drove her to the hospital and put her in a

To experience the Divine is to rest fully in God's love while we have an experience of the cross—an experience of freedom and liberation at all times of life, even in suffering, sickness, and death.

wheelchair, and as he was wheeling her in, she asked him to get a piece of paper and a pencil. You might think she was going to dictate her last will and testament. But she was thinking about her husband and her little children. Her husband did not know how to cook. She had done all the cooking all her life. She started dictating simple recipes to her husband so that he would be able to eat and feed the children. While dictating those recipes in the emergency room, she died. I have never felt sorry for my godmother. I envy her. I pray to her. I say, "Give me that spirit, give me that heart that can live so freely when I know I am going to die, when I know that everything is gone." She had just a short time to live, but she lived so fully. For her, death was a joke. Dictating recipes, she passed from this life to the next.

That for me was an insight into what the cross of Jesus is all about. It is not freedom from death. It is not freedom from suffering. It is not freedom from pain. It is the inner freedom that we experience in suffering, in pain, and in the face of death. And this freedom is available to us all. That is the Good News of Jesus Christ. To experience the Divine is to rest fully in God's love while we have an experience of the cross—an experience of freedom and liberation at all times of life, even in suffering, sickness, and death.

Are Your Possessions Enslaving or Freeing?

25

My tribal friends in India are on a perpetual honeymoon with God because the material things of this world do not matter to them. They do not have anything; therefore, they cherish everything.

One root of evil is the material things we crave. Another root of evil is the material things in our homes that we cling to—in American society, the stuff in our basements and attics. We collect and store things, and when we get old, we look at our children and our grandchildren and our nieces and nephews and see that they don't care that much about our stuff. After we die, they have a garage sale, and most of the stuff we cherished winds up in other people's basements and attics. What doesn't sell at the garage sale ends up on the curb or ultimately in the garbage.

Later, our children go to other people's garage sales and bring other people's stuff into their homes. And on it goes.

Whether evil is personal, familial, communal, national, or international, material things of this world are the root. It all begins with the material things we crave, the material things we cling to, the material things we gather, and the material things we hold on to without ever enjoying them.

We collect all these mementos, we put them on display, we look at them for a few days, and then we mostly forget about them. Of course, the rest of the time we spend putting alarm systems in our homes so that nobody will take these things. We don't look at them, and we don't enjoy them. But should something happen to any of these things, we are devastated. We are devastated because those things were "so precious." But for whom? We barely ever saw them, we never spent time with them, and we never really enjoyed them.

We become enslaved by our material possessions, and we lose our freedom. We look for better-paying jobs so we can clutter our houses with more stuff. We want to have more and better stuff than our neighbors, because we identify our self-worth with our possessions. Our addiction to possessions does not allow for any quality time with ourselves, our families, our friends, or the Divine. Lost in the mire of this material world, we lose sight of anything spiritual. We become so engrossed in our material possessions that we lose our identity as spiritual beings and our freedom to live the fullness of life.

Get rid of the material things in your home, and you will learn how to be free. In getting rid of material things, you are making space for the spiritual. If you give your stuff away as an individual, you make space for your personal spirituality. If you give it away as a family, your family will grow spiritually. If you do it as a community, you will grow as a faith community; and if you do it as a nation, you will truly become the land of the free and the brave. It begins there. It begins with liberation from these material things. It begins with not going to the latest sale at your favorite store. I am not saying you shouldn't buy something you really need or just like when there is a sale. But don't buy just *because* there is a sale. *I don't need it, but I got a good deal, so I bought three of them.* Or *I needed one, but I got three*—if that is the case, then give two to your neighbors right away. Having more than you need is a burden, not a blessing. You do not need three when you learn how to live with one. When you learn to live with the minimum, then you are free.

We tell a story in India of a man who wants enlightenment, to become a holy man and a mystic, so he goes to his teacher, the guru, who tells him, "Sell everything you own, give the money to the poor; then come to me, and I will help you." The man does exactly as his teacher says and comes back with nothing but a cloth that he wraps around his waist and another one that he wears when he washes the first one. That is all he possesses. The teacher tells him, "Good. Now go to that village, sit in meditation and pray, and the villagers will take care of you." So the man sits and prays and makes great progress in the spiritual life, and the village feels blessed by the presence of this holy man. People come from all around to learn from him.

One day, he takes that cloth that he wears around his waist, washes it, and puts it on the roof of a little hut to dry. Some rats appear and begin to eat holes in the cloth. The poor man is frustrated, so he goes to the villagers and says, "Please give me another piece of cloth, because the rats have eaten

We become so engrossed in our material possessions that we lose our identity as spiritual beings and our freedom to live the fullness of life.

this one." The villagers give him another cloth, and the rats attack that one too. This goes on day after day until the villagers say, "Look, we are poor. We cannot give you a new piece of cloth every day. Please take this cat; it will take care of the rats for you." So he takes the cat from them, and the next time he hangs that piece of cloth out to dry, it stays intact, because the cat has eaten all the rats.

But now the man has a cat, and the cat has to be fed, because there are no more rats. So the man goes to the villagers, and they give him milk for his cat, but after a few days they tell him, "We cannot afford to give you milk every day; please take this cow." So he takes the cow, and soon the cow needs somewhere to graze, and so the villagers give the man a plot of land. Then they give him a woman to take care of this land and the cow and the cat and him. A little while later, this holy man marries the woman, and they make a home together and live happily ever after.

How did all this start? When the rats attacked the cloth that he would wrap around himself and he accepted ownership of the cat. That seems reasonable, right? For better reasons, he got a cow, and for practical reasons, he obtained a field and married a woman. What happened to his spirituality? It was gone. His teacher came to the village after a few years to look for that man who had made such great progress in his spiritual life—and he found a man who was like everyone else. This mystic whose heart and spirit were free, soaring beyond the sacred boundaries and seeking ever new horizons, slowly but surely found himself being enslaved by his material possessions. St. Ignatius believed that the temptation to riches was the source of all other vices.

Lightening Our Load along the Journey

26

A college professor who was nearing retirement decided to clean out his basement. It was filled with boxes of notes and lesson plans for his classes that he had collected for decades. Box after box went out of his house and to the recycling center. One day, his wife went down into the basement and saw that it was still full of boxes. "What's going on?" she asked. "I thought you were cleaning out the basement." "Well," the professor said, "I made copies of everything I gave away, just in case."

Becoming free in order to make room for the spiritual in our lives begins with getting rid of the material possessions that weigh us down. When we look carefully and objectively at our lives, we will see that we do not need that much to make and keep us happy. For example, when people come for retreats, I ask them, "Are the things that you have brought with you meeting your needs and giving you comfort?" They say yes. Then I ask, "How many of the things that you have left at home do you really need? How much more than what you take on vacation, business trips, and retreats do you really need?" I am not saying that we should give away everything. There are some things we do need. But how much of what we have in our lives is really necessary? Asking and responding to this is the beginning of our freedom.

When I look at my life, I see that I collect things from time to time, and at some point I'll say, "Where did all this stuff come from?!" That is when I know that I have to get rid of it. Get rid of it! If you haven't used something for six months, give it away. If you haven't laid eyes on it in ages, pass it on to another. Yes, you work hard for the things you have, but I would like you to review very seriously the material things that you have in your home and your office and your life—the "extra" things first, then the "essential" things. Start with the basement and the attic. What do you *really* need? Consider this carefully.

If you want a relationship with God, you must make space in your life for the spiritual. In a church where I once served, we would call the last Sunday of every month "BAD Sunday." What was BAD Sunday? It was Basement-Attic Disposal Sunday—and it was wonderful. Everyone was invited to go into their basement and their attic and bring something they found there to church.

If you want a relationship with God, you must make space in your life for the spiritual.

I used to say to my older parishioners, "Unless the angel Gabriel visits, you will probably not need the baby things that you have stored in your basement. There are young people getting married, having their babies. These baby things are expensive. Bring them to church so that the young people can use them. What else do you have in your basement—the refrigerator that your mother-in-law gave you that you've always hated and never used but don't know how to get rid of? Mother-in-law is gone, but the refrigerator is still there. Bring it to church! It has never worked right, you've never used it, and so we'll get rid of it for you. If it needs to be thrown away, we'll do it for you. But get rid of it." And the people who participated would feel lighter and happier.

It will be good to think about the things you have collected and give them away. You have Goodwill, you have St. Vincent de Paul stores, you have recycling centers, or you can just throw these things in the trash. You will be lighter and happier. One of the members of my parish community, who is the director of religious education for the diocese, introduced BAD Mondays into the elementary schools. On the last Monday of every month, the children bring to school something they no longer use. In this way, they are put on the pathway of spiritual freedom early in life.

If you're looking to jump-start your spiritual growth, you can start by getting rid of the material things that you possess. How did Jesus respond to the first temptation in the desert? He said, "Man does not live by bread alone." He is telling us that material things are unimportant and that the only thing that matters is our relationship with God, our life-giving, all-sustaining experience of the Divine. That is what matters. Get rid of the material anchors in your life, and your journey into the river of the Divine will be lighter and freer.

27 Are We Enslaved by Things We Do Not Fully Enjoy?

When I joined the Jesuits, I brought with me a blazer that I had received on Prize Distribution Day in high school. On that same day, the same blazer was given to a classmate of mine who is now an international sports star; in fact, he is in *Guinness World Records* for his cricket career. The blazer was a prize for excellence in sports, and I had been a recipient along with one of the world's greatest cricketers. I didn't really wear the blazer when I entered the Jesuit novitiate, but I brought it with me so that, if I had the chance, I could show it to people.

Early in the novitiate, we were having a monthlong retreat, and the novice director was talking with us about attachments. I went to speak with him privately and said, "Today you were talking about this attachment idea, and it's something really important, but I think I need a little more time." My novice director was sitting at the edge of his seat, and he said, "What are you attached to?" When I said, "My blazer," he told me to go get it. So I went, got the key to the trunk room, got the blazer, and brought it to my novice director . . . and I was happy that my attachment was gone. Wrong! As soon as the retreat was over, I went to my novice director and said, "May I have that blazer back? I don't have another one." I could have gotten another blazer, but the truth is that I didn't want another blazer; I wanted *that* one. Unfortunately, he said that he had given it away and I would never see it again. It was my attachment, so he gave it away.

For many years, I fretted about that blazer. I longed for it. I missed it. Why? Probably because, like those poor sheep whose wool went into my blazer, I did not have any fun experiences with it. Bombay is so hot that you don't need a woolen blazer, so I really never used it. The only time I wore it was when I took a photo for my sports ID. Where did I keep it? In the trunk room. Did I show it to anyone? Not really. Did I talk about it? Not really. Did anybody know about it? Not really. I never enjoyed it, and so when it was taken away, I missed it. I really missed it.

If you give away something that you're attached to but you haven't enjoyed, it will haunt you for the rest of your life.

We are enslaved by people, places, and things that we do not fully enjoy. How do we free ourselves? By enjoying them. If you haven't enjoyed something and you are attached to it, do not give it away yet. If you do, it will haunt you forever. You will think of it often, fret over it, crave it. The thought of it won't leave you. The way to get rid of material things is by enjoying them, being grateful for them, and then giving them away: good-bye, gone.

I always like to tell this story of my nephew, who took great delight in chocolate when he was little. My sister would give him a box of chocolates and say, "Go share some with everybody." So he would come to me, and we would play a game. I would say, "Which one should I take?" He would say, "Any one." I would then say, "Which one do you like?" He would point: "This one." "May I have that one?" I would ask. He would say, "Yes, please have it."

This is an only child who can give away the piece of chocolate that he likes the most. How? Well, to understand, you would have to see him eating a chocolate. One time, I took him to visit a family with me, and the mother said, "Oh, you like chocolates? Eat, eat." She brought a whole jar of the treats and set them before him. Now, my nephew did not pick up the first chocolate in the jar and eat it. No. With his big eyes, he looked for his favorite one. Then he picked it up, unwrapped it carefully, and began licking it, savoring the taste. You would feel hungry simply looking at him, because he was enjoying it so much. I asked the woman, "You won't mind if he eats the whole jar? Let's just leave him alone and visit." I knew exactly what my nephew would do. He finished his piece of chocolate and went to play. He didn't want another one. Why? Because he enjoyed that single chocolate to the last lick. Similarly, once when he was not well, the doctor told him he couldn't have chocolate for three months. Did he miss it? No, because he had enjoyed it when he had it.

This is not only true of my nephew and his chocolate. With his toys he's the same way. He's an only child, but he wants everybody else to enjoy his toys, and if they are given away, he doesn't miss them. This is not because he is sure of getting more toys. He can give things away because he enjoys them, and when they're gone he doesn't miss them.

Places, people, things—enjoy them so you are not possessed by them. Why is it that we are so attached to our homes? Because we haven't fully enjoyed them. If we truly enjoy where we live, if we say, "I am grateful for this beautiful house; I am grateful for all the wonderful memories," then we can move on when we are called to do so.

We are enslaved by people, places, and things that we do not fully enjoy. How do we free ourselves? By enjoying them.

Our memories always stay with us, as do the warmth and the energy of things—not just our photographs. Think of the many people today who spend so much time taking pictures and videos of their children but never really look at their children. They look at photographs and videos. Now they even put the pictures on the Internet and have the rest of us look at them. You never see the actual child, but pictures— yes, you see lots of pictures.

If you have something and never enjoy it, and someone takes it from you, what happens? Are you happy that they're enjoying something that you were not quite finished with? No—you will not be able to get over the loss. You will not be able to get over it because you haven't finished enjoying this thing that was taken from you. The attachment is still there. But if you have spent time enjoying what you have and are grateful to have had it, you will not be distressed if somebody takes it away from you.

So if there's some material thing you once had and still miss in your life, you may be enslaved by something you didn't fully enjoy. But if you haven't gotten over losing it, you don't have to bring the thing back to free yourself from the attachment. What you can do is talk to what you have lost, in your imagination, in your fantasy, knowing that this thing will probably never come back to you. I can talk to my sports blazer—I can tell it how much I appreciate it and then let it go. It was wonderful, I'm grateful for the gift of it, but I can move on; I don't miss it now. In your imagination, in your heart, experience your attachments in full, talk to them, be in relationship with them, be grateful to have had them in your life at all, and then move on—knowing that with a God of infinite possibilities, there are other wonderful surprises to be enjoyed. Move on knowing that as someone created in the image and likeness of the Divine, you don't really need any of these things to be the complete, whole, self-contained being that you are.

This works as well with the people you have lost without fully enjoying them. When people in your life die and you haven't told them that you love them or haven't shared enough of yourself with them, you will miss them, you will always be attached to them, but you can still talk to them. Appreciate what they did and what they've given you and what they meant to you. If you do, then you can let go.

A Beginner's Mind 28

The Buddhists talk a lot about having a beginner's mind. They believe that the beginner's mind has many possibilities, while the expert's mind has few. This is a beautiful way to approach life. Having a beginner's mind means doing things as if you were doing them for the first time. When you meet your wife or your husband at home every day, have a beginner's mind, and it is as if you are meeting this person for the first time. Do you remember the first time you met? The wonder, the charm . . . People need to look at one another with that same freshness, with that beginner's mind, to reengage the spark of their first meeting. We all want to work out our relationships and grow in our relationships. We need to be able to pick up a spark and then get the fire going again.

It works the same way in your vocation. If you're a teacher, teach as if you were teaching for the first time, with that freshness, with that spontaneity, with that passion. Or if you're a doctor, or a nurse, or a therapist, engage with those you serve as if they were your very first patients. Or if you're a coach, coach as if you were coaching your first team.

If you look at your life and relationships as ever new and changing, then you cannot get attached to anything. You give yourself fully to what you have at the present moment, because it will keep changing. You wait in anticipation for the spirit of the Lord to hover over this moment and bring forth a new and more beautiful creation. You are led from the 1 percent that is physical to the 99 percent that is spiritual—the spiritual that explodes into infinite possibilities.

They believe that the beginner's mind has many possibilities, while the expert's mind has few.

The beginner's mind is a mental and spiritual discipline. When you apply it, you minimize or even free yourself from routine thoughts and perceptions and expectations. This opens you up, enabling something new to be born or something long forgotten to be rediscovered. It opens you up to experience the Divine in all sorts of surprising places, and it can help open you to an ever-bigger God.

So when you eat, eat as if you were eating for the first time; when you pray, pray as if you were praying for the first time. When you receive the Eucharist, receive it as if you were receiving it for the first time. That's when life has meaning under all circumstances until our last breath.

The Enslaving Illusion of Love 29

Love is one of the greatest illusions that people have. This illusion of love is often the biggest obstacle to our relationship with God and to our greater and deeper experience of the Divine.

Reflect for a moment on the story of the couple who were so madly in love that every parent who had a teenage child would point to them and say, "If you want to know what love is, look at that couple." One day the man died. The woman was so devastated that on his tombstone she had engraved in bold letters, "The light of my life is gone." People would go there to show their children that inscription and to talk about this ideal couple and how they loved each other. People also stopped by to console the woman, and one man stopped by often. He fell in love with the woman, and eventually she fell in love with him, and soon she wanted to get married again. But that tombstone was an embarrassment. They went to their pastor for advice. He said, "Let it be; don't worry. You have written, 'The light of my life is gone.' Just add 'I have struck another match.'"

Abraham Lincoln once said that everyone is as happy as he or she chooses to be. Happiness, therefore, is an inner choice. When someone loves you, that person does not make you happy but makes you aware of the source of your happiness within you. Therefore, when someone you love rejects you, or goes away or dies, that person does not take your happiness with him or her.

> *When someone loves you, that person does not make you happy but makes you aware of the source of your happiness within you.*

When we cling to the love of another person or are dependent on it for our happiness, we become enslaved to that relationship. We fool ourselves by believing that our happiness comes from that person instead of from the river of divine life and because we are the beloved of God. Such a relationship is not a truly unconditional loving relationship. True love lets me freely be who I am.

God's most precious gifts are sometimes the very obstacles that stand in the way of our deepening our relationship with the Divine. Sometimes our relationships, even good ones, prevent us from moving to a higher spiritual level. Ramakrishna, one of the great Indian sages, tells this story:

There was a holy man who wandered the forests, always lost in the presence of God. Through his wanderings, he came to the city one day and found a young man, a wonderful man, and said to him, "Why are you wasting your time here? Come with me into the forest, and I will show you how to experience God, peace, and happiness." The young man said, "I can't do that. I have a wife who loves me dearly; she would be devastated if I went away. I have children who depend on me. They love me so much. Our family is so close to one another. There is so much love in this family. I cannot just leave them and go." The holy man said, "This is an illusion. It is a figment of your imagination. They don't love you the way you think they do. You don't love them the way you think you do." And the young man replied, "Of course I do." So the holy man said, "Let's test this."

The holy man suggested, "I will give you this little potion. When you go home, drink it, and you will fall down as if you are dead, but you will be aware of everything that is going on. I promise you that shortly I will come and revive you." The young man agreed. He went home, took that potion, and fell down as if he were dead. His wife was the first one to find him, and she began screaming and yelling and could not be consoled. "This husband of mine," she cried, "I love him so much. Why did God take him away so soon and so quickly?" His children also could not be consoled. All the neighbors were in the house trying to help the family. They were also talking about how much they loved this man. And the young man was thinking, *I hope the holy man comes now, because he would then see for himself how much I am loved and cared for.*

The holy man appeared. He asked, "What happened?" The wife said, "This husband of mine—I loved him so much and now he is gone, and I do not know what I am going to do without him." The children said the same thing. The neighbors were talking about him too. The holy man announced, "I can revive this man. I have this little potion. If I put it into his mouth, he will come back to life." And everyone stopped crying and looked forward in hope. "But there is one condition for this potion to work. One of you has to take half of it, and you will die. I am sure you love him very much and will have no problem doing this."

The wife spoke first. She said, "What is a home without a mother? This man does not know how to cook. This man will not be able to take care of the children." So, she said, she could not possibly take the potion. The children said, "Papa lived a good life. God will reward him. We are young and have our own lives to lead." The neighbors had their own families, so no one among them was willing to take the potion. The holy man revived the young man, and without turning back, the young man followed the holy man into the forest.

God's most precious gifts are sometimes the very obstacles that stand in the way of our deepening our relationship with the Divine.

Now, I am not suggesting that you leave all your loved ones and go into the forest. What I am saying is that you should look at this great illusion of love for what it is. Don't give your loved ones and friends more importance, more value than they have. Jesus said, "Unless you hate your father and your mother and your brothers and sisters, you cannot be my disciple." I am not saying that you should stop loving your family. Jesus did not say that. Jesus said, "Love them with all your heart and all your soul. Love them like you love God. Love them like you love yourself." Love them, but know that you have to let go of them at the same time so that you will be able to follow God totally and unconditionally. This is something that we all need to think about. We all have to face this illusion in some manner, and the consequences of how we do so are very real.

When my mother died, all of us at home were worried about our father. He had spent forty-seven years married to my mother and was very devoted to her. We wondered if my father would die now that the love of his life was gone. But he didn't; he survived. He lived for twelve years after her death. Not only did he live, but he was fully alive. He was fully present to life. Of course he missed my mother. Of course he talked about my mother. But her death did not devastate him; it did not kill him.

When people die, we miss them and we cry for them, but if we truly loved them and freely enjoyed them, we cry because we're happy. The tears are tears of happiness, because their lives were a gift to us and we remember the happy moments. Because we fully enjoyed them, we are free to let them go on the physical level and stay connected to them on the spiritual level.

This is true even in our relationship with the Divine. One of St. Ignatius's axioms is "Pray as if everything depended on God and work as if everything depended on you." What St. Ignatius is saying is that we need to give ourselves fully to the task, in which *God* is laboring, and trust fully in the Divine. This reflects a childlike approach rather than a childish approach. In this relationship, we are free to be who we are, and God is free to be divine. This relationship is one of freeing love.

30 Original Sin, Reconsidered

In the Catholic Church on Ash Wednesday, we receive ashes on our foreheads. What are those ashes? For me, they are a reminder that God is indeed tattooed upon my body. The ashes on my forehead are a symbol of my being tattooed with the Divine, as certain tribal people of India are tattooed. Ash Wednesday is a great moment in the church's liturgical year. It marks the beginning of Lent—forty days to celebrate that tattooing. It is an invitation to sing and dance, to be free, to celebrate life *in the midst of* suffering, sickness, and death. It is not so much about remembering that I am dust, and unto dust I shall return. It is certainly not about remembering that I am a miserable wretch, a sinner who is going to hell, and whatever I do I am doomed for my sinfulness, and poor Jesus had to come into this world to die for my sins.

My Jesus didn't die for my sins. My Jesus died as the greatest sign of love ever expressed for us. My Jesus died to bring a new knowledge and a new consciousness to humanity. My Jesus died because he was different from the other religious people of his time. My Jesus died because he did not give a damn for the well of religion. My Jesus died because he spent his time with social and religious outcasts, tax collectors, prostitutes, and sinners, promising them that the kingdom of God belonged to them. My Jesus died because he came to destroy the temple. Jesus died to give us the knowledge that God is within us and that when God created us, he created us like himself. When God created us, he put his breath into us. You and I are the breath of God. You and I are not sinners with original sin.

What is original sin? Is it the root of all evil? If you were from India, you would say yes and no. The root of evil is original sin, but how do we understand original sin?

I like to look at original sin as a choice that introduced ignorance. Adam and Eve ate the forbidden fruit out of a false idea of what it means to be divine. They were ignorant of who they truly were. Not realizing that we live in the breath of God, not knowing that we are spiritual beings, not knowing that we are divine—this is the root of evil. Jesus came to give us this knowledge and remind us of our identity. He came to remind us that at our baptism, the heavens opened up, and God addressed us, saying, "You are my beloved child. I am well pleased with you, my favor rests on you, my delight is in you." If we truly believe that we are children of God, then we recognize that we are divine heirs and that the gifts of God are our rightful and free inheritance.

Discovering our true identity in God is the beginning of knowledge. Adam and Eve were without this knowledge; Jesus gave us this knowledge when he prayed, not only for those whom God had given him but also for all, "that all of them may be one, Father, just as you are in me

If you don't worship God in your heart, you cannot experience him in church. If you don't experience the Divine inside you, you won't find God anywhere.

and I am in you" (John 17:21). Knowledge is discovering our identity, with Jesus, in the very being and essence of the Divine. Original sin is the state of being unaware of that true identity. The end of ignorance is finding that divine connection and that interconnectedness with the whole of creation: "You are in me and I am in you." Jesus preached a God who is spirit and truth, and if you don't worship God in your heart, you cannot experience him in church. If you don't experience the Divine inside you, you won't find God anywhere.

Confession, 31
Celebration of Divine
Presence

The Catholic Church, Christendom, society at large—they all talk about the idea of confession. What is confession? It all depends on how you look at it. Confession, to me, is not a Laundromat, where you go and dump all your dirt, get clean, and then go away happy. If you look at the Bible, confession begins with an encounter, an experience of God. I come to confession to talk about this great experience that I have had. Confession is a time to focus on *God*, not my sins.

Religion teaches that repentance is a necessary condition to experiencing God's love. Jesus, on the other hand, invited people to experience the Good News—the good news that we are loved totally and unconditionally. Repentance, therefore, becomes a consequence and not a condition of God's love.

Take Moses, for example. When did Moses realize that he was a sinner? He was there with the burning bush and began to draw closer, and he heard the voice of God calling him and saying, "The place where you stand is holy ground." When God confirmed Moses' mission, Moses hid his face and stuttered, "You know I can't even speak." What prompted this confession? Not his weakness in speaking but the fact that he had encountered God in the burning bush.

Repentance, therefore, becomes a consequence and not a condition of God's love.

Look at the story of Peter and the miraculous catch of fish in Luke 5. When Peter encountered God in Jesus with the miraculous catch of fish, he went facedown on the ground and exclaimed, "Depart from me, for I am a sinful man." That's when Jesus said that he would make Peter a fisher of men. While Peter confessed by his word and his life that Jesus was "Master," Mary Magdalene's confession was "Rabboni," and Thomas's was "My Lord and my God."

So what is confession? Confession is acknowledging the wonderful God whom I have just encountered and acknowledging that I am aware of my own shortcomings and weaknesses, which are obstacles to deepening my relationship with God and being able to share this experience with the rest of the world. This awareness is a *consequence* of my encounter, my experience of God, not a *condition* for the Divine's presence.

When I go to confession, I talk to the priest about the wonderful God whom I have encountered and experienced since my last confession. Then I talk about how everything in life can help me grow and respond to my divine experiences. And I am thankful for the self-awareness that these experiences have brought. I am thankful for the repentance that naturally flows in me as a result of this awareness. When I confess, it is the Divine's presence and unconditional love for me that I acknowledge and celebrate. Confession in its truest sense is a celebration of God's love. Every time I experience God in a new or bigger way, I need to run to confession.

Living in the Here and Now

32

After visiting the doctor, a man called his wife, crying. His wife asked, "What's the matter, honey?" He said, "Well, the doctor has given me these pills, and I have to take one each day for the rest of my life." And his wife asked, "So why are you upset?" He answered, "He has given me just four pills." If you were that man and had just four days to live, how would you live your life?

To live fully and freely, we need to accept the transitoriness of life. In the popular American understanding, there is no such thing as transitoriness. Everything is permanent. Everything is everlasting. Everyone is going to live forever. But the reality is that nothing in this world is permanent; nothing is here forever. Life is in constant flux; everything is constantly changing. You never step into the same river twice. Every time you meet a person, you are really meeting for the first time, because you both have changed since you last met. While you are holding on to your children, they are changing. While you are holding on to your parents and your loved ones, they too are changing. While you are holding on to your possessions, you are changing. The relationship that you have today is not the one you had yesterday and is not the one you will have tomorrow.

When you try to hold on to that which is constantly changing, you open yourself to frustration and disappointment. In the East, there is a saying that "a river keeps pure by flowing; a holy man keeps holy by going"—going deeper into the mystery of life to find a deeper consciousness of his identity in the Divine. In the midst of the transitoriness of life, the holy man seeks the one constant, the Divine he can find only in the here and now.

A Zen master was asked, "What is the secret of your life and your mysticism?" He said, "Every morning, I get up with a feeling that this might be my last day." Then he was asked, "Doesn't everyone know that?" The master said, "They know it; I feel it." If today is your last day, how do you want to live it? Do you still want to be angry with people who hurt you? Do you still want to hold on to that resentment? Do you still want to cling to all those things? If you had five minutes to live and one telephone call to make, who would you make it to, what would you tell them, and why are you waiting? You may not get another chance. To live fully in the now is to live as if this were your last day.

To live fully and freely, we need to accept the transitoriness of life.

Here's another way to live fully in the now, to live fully while in the midst of the transitoriness of life. Live as if you were in the presence of a striking cobra. When you are in the presence of this deadly, poisonous snake, you are not thinking about your sins or about the great things you did in life.

You are not thinking about your wealth, because there is no point. You are not thinking about what people will say and think about you. You are not thinking about your power and authority. You are fully in the now. Just think for a moment. This present moment is part of every moment from the beginning of time. This present moment is part of every moment until the end of time. This present moment is eternal time. The chair that you are sitting on, the ground that your feet are touching is part of everywhere. When you are living life fully in the now, fully in the here, you are living the eternal life, here and now.

We have another story in our Indian tradition, of a man who was being chased by a tiger. The fellow ran and ran until he reached a well. He jumped into the well and landed on a tree limb that was jutting out into the middle of the well. He looked up. The tiger was waiting for him at the top of the well. He looked down, and he saw poisonous snakes. He looked around him, and it was the fruit season. He stretched out his hand and began to taste and enjoy a ripe fruit. Now, think about this. This is meaningful psychology and spirituality and a wonderful way to live. Just because there is a tiger above me, just because there are snakes down below, why should I deprive myself of the beauty and the gift of the moment?

How often we are afraid of the tigers that are waiting for us. *Oh no, there's a tiger waiting for me over there—a tiger called my mother-in-law's upcoming visit, my credit card bill, my overattachment to food, my big presentation at work this week, that fight I had with my sister, my child's misbehavior, my love of power and self-importance, my spouse's diagnosis . . .* But you know what?

While you are sitting here thinking about the tiger over there, your body is here. Your mind is there and your body is here. You are not whole; you are fading in and out of yourself. You cannot really enjoy the gift of the present because you are thinking about that tiger. Your mind will not allow you to live in the moment. It either regrets the past or is anxious about the future. And when the tiger comes upon you, you find that it is not what you expected, and you think, *Why did I waste all that time worrying about the tiger?* And the fruit season is over.

Now, suppose when you confront the tiger, it eats you. You still have a choice: you can be eaten up having enjoyed the fruit, or you can be eaten up not having enjoyed the fruit. Better to eat the fruit, enjoy the moment, and be eaten up. Live life—live life to the full.

Are You Part of a Vertical World or a Horizontal World?

33

The Gospel of John famously opens with the Greek word *Logos*. It says that in the beginning was Logos, and Logos was with God, and Logos was God. A common translation for *Logos* is "word." If we translate *Logos* as "word," we live in a vertical world. If we translate *Logos* as "meaning," as some do, then we live in a horizontal world.

Let me try to explain this. In a vertical world, I find my identity and my place in the world from God and from everyone who represents God. If I'm Catholic, then God is represented by the church, the pope, cardinals, bishops, theologians, priests, elders, parents—all of these people tell me who I am and what is expected of me in life.

As a reaction to this vertical world, which is very structured, people began to rebel and to live for themselves. The "God, God, God" maxim of the vertical world became "Me, me, me." Self-interest and self-gain became the deciding factors for all aspects of life.

In a horizontal world, which came about in response to the disasters of the "Me, me, me" world, I begin to look for meaning. I find my identity, my role in this life, and what is expected of me from within myself. I'm not looking for somebody else to tell me who I am and what is expected of me. Nor am I living a selfish life, but I try to live a meaningful life.

If we want to know what kind of world we're living in, we can ask ourselves some questions: Where am I? Where am I at this point in my life? Am I looking for some external authority in my life, in my family, or in my church to tell me who I am and what is expected of me? To tell me where I come from and where I am going, to tell me about my beginning and my end? Or am I living a self-centered or selfish life? Or do I look into myself and say, "This is who I am, this is where I come from, and this is where I am going"? Do I say, "Whatever anybody else may tell me, I own and take responsibility for what I have found within"? If your experience is the first, you are living in a vertical world; if you answer the last, you are living in a horizontal world. So are you part of a vertical world or a horizontal world? Or are you both, part vertical and part horizontal?

In my case, I depend on the experience of tradition; I depend on the wisdom of elders to help me find out who I am and what is expected of me in life—that's vertical. However, at the same time, I depend on them but do not become dependent on them—that's horizontal. I consult them in their wisdom, and then I am able to integrate that wisdom into myself and give it a personal expression in my daily life. Based on the wisdom of tradition and the experiences of elders—or whatever else I need and find—I discover who I am and decide what is expected of me in life. That's probably the ideal scenario—learning to take the best of the vertical and the best of the horizontal and live a meaningful life.

The "Me" and the "I"   34

The psychologist Viktor Frankl wrote that Western society has experienced three phases of understanding. The first phase began in the Middle Ages, when everything was about God. There was God in the morning, God in the afternoon, and God in the evening. God gave me these children, it's God's plan that I have this illness, and it's God's will that this person died. It is God's blessing that I got this wonderful job and God's will that I lost the job. Everything is God's will, God's plan.

That phase lasted until the 1960s, when there was a reaction to this understanding of God—and to the vertical world where we had to look outside and above ourselves to find out who we were and what was expected of us in life. The 1960s saw a reaction to institutions, structures, and authority. We had the hippie movement, where everything was about self-actualization and me, me, me: Why should I care about anybody else; what's in it for me? How can I profit from it? How am I going to be a better person? How am I going to be a happier person? I don't care about anything or anyone else except as it relates to me. Everything revolves around me and is about me.

The second phase was all about "me." Frankl said that many people live in a world populated by one. This is the consequence of the "Me, me, me" experience. The only person of any importance, the only person who really exists, is me. When you live in a world with a population of one, you experience alienation. People say, "Okay, if it's all about you, fine." Then all of a sudden, you find yourself alone. When you are alienated, you become depressed. When you feel depressed, you try to overcome your depression through alcohol, drugs, sex, and a lot of other wasteful activities. Are you a workaholic, working to escape being alone, giving all you have at your workplace, and spending the weekend compulsively cleaning the house? Do you shop impetuously? Or are you one of those who cannot turn off the TV yet complain that there is nothing worth watching? Do you hit the casinos and gamble to run away from being alone? Or do you just look for people constantly because you are afraid of being alone? Remember that loneliness haunts places where crowds gather. People living in a world of one try to fill their lives with meaningless activities, and of course this doesn't help their depression. Fleeting and sometimes serious thoughts of suicide begin to surface in these people. For me, suicide is not just taking one's life; it is also choosing to stop living. There are many people who have committed suicide, in this sense, at the age of sixteen and are still waiting to be buried at sixty. They're not really alive; they simply exist, moving like ghosts from one day to the next.

Today we are in the third phase. People are looking for meaning anywhere and everywhere, and when they find it, they find the Divine and they find themselves. I find God and I find me. Of course, this is not the "me" me. I find the "I," the big Self, not the small self. What's the difference between the "me" and the "I"? The "me" is always changing. The "me" is happy one day and sad the next. The "me" is successful one day, depressed another day, and a failure the next. The "I" never changes. It's constant. The "I" is the image and likeness of God, created good and beautiful. The "I" is the breath of God. When God created human beings, he made man and woman out of clay and put into that clay his own breath. That breath of life is the "I." God saw that the "I" is very good, that it is eternal and never changes. The "me," however, keeps changing. When you are looking for meaning, you live less and less with the "me" and more and more with the "I."

Most people don't know who they really are. Are you your body? Your body changes from year to year—this is the current model; last year's model is gone. If you don't believe your body changes every year, at least you believe that the body you have today is not the one you had as a child. The "I" never changes, so you are not your body.

People are looking for meaning anywhere and everywhere, and when they find it, they find the Divine and they find themselves.

Are you your feelings? Your feelings are changing all the time. Are you your thinking? Your thoughts are changing all the time. Are you the incredible work you are doing? That work is not a constant; once you're dead, chances are nobody will care about your work. Are you your relationships? The person you are in relationship with is constantly changing, the dynamic of the relationship is constantly changing, and you are changing too.

So who am I? I like what Paul says in his letter to the Galatians (3:28). He writes that in our relationship with God through Christ Jesus, we are neither male nor female, Jew nor Gentile, slave nor free—that's the "I." I'm not even my maleness. Beyond being a male, there is something else. Beyond being an Indian, there is something else. Beyond my body, my emotions, my thinking, my personal relationships—beyond all of this, there is something else. And that's the "I." When I encounter that "I," I will be free. When I live by that "I," then my experience in this life will change. When I experience that "I," I will finally begin to live.

Our Stolen Search for Meaning

Most people in the first world have basic necessities like food, shelter, and clothing. We have all that we need, plus some. We have air-conditioning when it's hot. We have heating when it's cold. We have one car, maybe two, and probably two or three television sets. We have a personal computer, a cell phone, a microwave, and a washing machine, and our lives have become comfortable. Yet so many people do not have meaning.

Viktor Frankl offers an interesting insight into this situation. He suggests that there are three axioms that can help us understand how to live life meaningfully. The first is that life has meaning under all circumstances until our last breath. The second axiom states that we all have an innate will to meaning, our strongest motivation for living and acting. Simply put, this second axiom means that if we don't have a reason to live, then we'll die. On this level, it could be a bad reason, it could be the wrong reason, it could be an evil reason, but if we don't have a reason to live, we'll die. The third axiom, according to Frankl, is that we have the freedom to find meaning, and the meaning that we discover is *the* meaning of life, the existential meaning that we find through asking the existential questions: who am I, where do I come from, where am I going, and what is the purpose of my life?

When we examine our lives in today's world, we find we have a lot to live *on* but very little to live *for*. Capitalist society has robbed people of the search for meaning by convincing them that happiness will be found in the next purchase, the next drink, the next extravaganza. But consumerism and the pleasures of life do not satisfy the human spirit, as today's multitudes of quietly desperate or desperately longing people can attest. When the well of religion offers dogmas, liturgies, and rote prayers without engaging the heart, it also robs people of an experience of the Divine and fails to satisfy the spirit. With Mary Magdalene, we can say, "They have taken away my Lord, and I do not know where they have put him."

By robbing us of the search for meaning, religion and society have robbed us of the will to live and the freedom to attain the ultimate meaning in life. This is like the man who went to the supermarket to buy a piece of meat. With the meat he was given a recipe book. When he came out of the supermarket, someone stole the meat. The man stood laughing at the thief as he ran away. He shouted at him, "Fool! You've got the meat, but I've got the recipe book!" We have a wonderful recipe book, but religion has stolen the meat. What use is a recipe book without the meat?

> *When the well of religion offers dogmas, liturgies, and rote prayers without engaging the heart, it also robs people of an experience of the Divine and fails to satisfy the spirit.*

Since society and religion give people a means to no end, people must find it for themselves. Some find it in social causes, others in the arts and culture; some find it in their professions, or in their family life, while still others in their quest for meaning are drawn to cults, and even terrorist groups. When social causes, arts and culture, business, family, cults, and terrorist groups become ends in themselves, however, they become an obstacle to attaining the ultimate goal and meaning in life. Slowly we make these things *the* meaning of our lives, and they become lesser gods of sorts. They prevent us from encountering the eternal "I" that is our identity in the Divine and our interconnectedness with the rest of humanity and the whole of creation.

36 What Do You Want on Your Tombstone?

There is a group of nuns in India who declare humorously how great their devotion to Mary is. They have assigned titles from the Litany of Our Lady to different sisters in their community. One sister is called The Cause of Our Joy. When life is gloomy, dull, and filled with anxiety, this sister walks into the room, and before anyone realizes it everyone is chatting away; her humor fills the room with laughter, and soon the dark clouds seem to melt away, making room for joy. This sister is now a missionary in some far-off country, and wherever she goes her joyful spirit is contagious. The inscription on her tombstone might read: Here lies The Cause of Our Joy!

Another sister is called The Tower of Wisdom. Everyone looks to this sister for her wisdom to find a way out of seemingly impossible situations. She attracts people who seek solutions to the difficult and painful times in their lives.

The community is also home to The Virgin Most Afflicted. She complains constantly that no one likes her, no one seems to understand her, and no one cares. Nothing seems to be good enough for her.

What about you—what would sum up who you are? What are you living for? What is the purpose of your life? There is another way of asking these questions: what would you want engraved on your tombstone?

What do you want on your tombstone—not in the future, but right now? Give it some thought. Help those who will prepare your tombstone: write out now what you want it to say. Show it to your family, maybe even carve it out and keep it ready. How would you sum up your life in just a few words? If you live on the level of meaning, you will have no difficulty with this.

Our tombstones sum up the story of our lives. They reflect the legacy that we leave behind. They are a way for us to reflect on the meaning and message of our lives. The inscription on the tombstone of a young man who died reads: "His life taught us how to live; his death, how to die!" This young man had lived his life to the full, and his death became just a passing to the fullness of eternal life. His tombstone remains an inspiration for the rest of us.

What would sum up who you are? What are you living for? What is the purpose of your life?

So what would you like engraved on your tombstone? How would you wish to sum up the story and meaning of your life? If you decide this now, you begin to clarify that meaning, and in all likelihood you will live accordingly so that your tombstone becomes a self-fulfilling prophecy.

37 Life Does Not Owe Us Pleasure—It Offers Us Meaning

If you accept that our strongest motivation for living and acting is an innate will to meaning—in other words, that we'll die without some reason to live—then this will to meaning *will* come in opposition to the will to pleasure. Freud talked a lot about pleasure. He said that if people do not have pleasure in life, they will die. He was smart. Think about what we see on our television programs and read in our newspapers and magazines—all the talk in our culture about the pleasures that "make life worth living." The message we hear is "When life has no pleasure, you will die. So buy this, do that, believe in this . . ."

Pleasure comes in different forms. Take my students. They want to have everything easy: "Give me an A. I won't do the work, but give me an A anyway. I will show up in class, so give me an A." They want ease and pleasure. Once they are sixteen, it's "Give me a car, and let me continue this life of pleasure and ease and comfort."

But life does not owe us pleasure—it offers us meaning. The will to pleasure is a dead end. Life is not pleasurable. Any mature person, any person with common sense, will tell you that life is full of suffering. Birth is suffering. Death is suffering. Meeting people is suffering. Separating is suffering. Saying hello is suffering. Saying good-bye is suffering. Life is full of pain. Life does not owe us pleasure; it offers us meaning. Pleasure is a by-product of meaningful activity.

You can apply this to your work situation. For some people, going to work every day is not pleasurable. But if you have meaningful work, you will always come back satisfied and generally happy. There is meaning in bringing up children, though the work is not always pleasurable. (That's why it's nice to be a grandmother or an uncle, because you can send them back.) If you find meaning in bringing up your children, you will find pleasure. The work may not always be fun, but ultimately it will always be satisfying. Life does not owe us pleasure; it offers us meaning.

We all have the freedom to find meaning in life, and this meaning is the *big* meaning. It's the meaning I have to find. It's not what religion tells me. It's not what my parents tell me. It's not what the teachers or the sages or the presidents or the CEOs tell me. It's not what anybody else tells me. As a human being, a creation of God, I am invited to find my own meaning.

Pleasure is a by-product of meaningful activity.

38 Do You React or Respond to Life?

S tephen Covey, in *The Seven Habits of Highly Effective People*, shares an experience that he once had while traveling on the New York subway. Imagine you are riding the subway early one morning, and everybody appears to be comfortable—people are drinking their coffee, reading their newspapers and magazines, working on their laptops, talking on their cell phones. Everything is normal and peaceful. At each station, a few people get off, a few people get on, everything is calm and sedate, until the train stops at a particular station and a man walks onto your train car with his little children. He finds seats for them and then sits down in a reflective mood. While he is in deep meditation, the children begin to run up and down the aisle, screaming and shouting, running all over the train car.

How do you feel? Are you mad at the man? Why are you mad? You are perhaps thinking, *This man should take care of his children in public. If he does not know how to take care of children, why did he have them in the first place?* Are you mad at the children for making so much noise? *Spoiled kids!* you might think. You notice there is no mother. Now you might be thinking, *I bet the mother left this man with these undisciplined children.* See yourself going up to this irresponsible father and confronting him, saying, "Excuse me, sir, would you mind tending to your children? They're being so disruptive, and I think everybody is getting a little upset." The man looks up at you and says, "Two hours ago these children lost their mother in the hospital. She just died, and ever since then I have been trying to explain to them the death of their mother, and their only reaction is this."

Now how do you feel? The children are still jumping up and down, screaming and shouting. But now you feel terrible. You feel guilty. You feel sorry for the man, you feel sorry for the children, and you feel bad about their mother. You might even feel upset with yourself for feeling negatively about the father and his children.

I give you this example to demonstrate the power of our beliefs. Emotions are not caused by situations. Emotions are caused by our *beliefs* about situations, beliefs that color our perception and our understanding of events. In this example, the children are still jumping up and down and shouting, but some of us have moved from being upset to feeling sad, compassionate, and concerned. Others may still feel angry, because they believe that children should always behave in public. Beliefs cause emotions that trigger behavior. If we feel angry about a situation and react in anger, it is because we have angry beliefs about it. If we feel compassionate, it is because we have compassionate beliefs.

Situations in themselves do not produce feelings. It is our perception of the situation that makes us feel good or bad. Just as situations cannot make us happy or sad, another person cannot make us feel happy or sad. We choose to be happy or sad. If we seek greater freedom in our lives, we need to be objective and rational about the power of our beliefs versus the power of situations. *We* control our emotions. When we live in freedom, we choose the way we respond rather than let our automatic destructive reactions get the better of us.

Now you might ask, "Okay, but *how* do I do this? How do I choose to respond when I am under pressure, when I have been taught to fear or fight, when the situation seems 'bad' to me?" The "PQR formula" can help us live freely in stressful, anxious, or depressing situations. We *pause* to *question* how we would like to *respond* rather than react and live to regret our negative reaction. Let me try to explain what I mean by *react*: You push; I shove. Without thinking, I shove. This is my reaction. It is immediate and disconnected from my higher Self, the constant "I," and the meaning of my life. My reaction is an imprisoned effect. This is not freedom. By applying the PQR formula, however, I can *respond*. I pause (find myself in the situation), question (How does this situation relate to the meaning of my life? How do I wish to respond given a world of infinite possibilities?), and then respond (a freely chosen action—not a reaction). Responding rather than reacting helps us live freely and in greater

Situations in themselves do not produce feelings. It is our perception of the situation that makes us feel good or bad.

harmony with our true identity in every situation. It helps us grab hold of the freedom we seek in order to enter into the river of divine life.

So What Is a Belief?   **39**

Whatever it is we might want to change in our life, we first have to change our beliefs. When I say "beliefs" here, I mean that which we believe to be true in our gut even though we may deny it in our head. For example, I may proclaim that I am not a racist but cannot even think of one of my children marrying someone from another ethnic group. Or I say I believe in an all-loving God but pray for the conversion of all those who do not practice my religion. Some people think that one's beliefs cannot be changed, that they are what they are. But beliefs are learned, and therefore they can be unlearned.

We are not born with beliefs. Consider the life of a child. A child doesn't come with a set of beliefs. A child will play with anyone; a child will go and do anything. A child knows few differences. In fact, according to Carl Jung, a little child, as the innocent, thinks that he or she is still in paradise, the center of the world, where needs are provided for and everything is magical. The child develops beliefs when exposed to the reactions of the significant people in his or her surroundings. Beliefs are learned and therefore can be unlearned, and new beliefs can be learned. In a sense, we are constantly brainwashing or manipulating or reprogramming ourselves—why not do it for a positive change?

Let's take our beliefs about death, for example. Is death good or bad, happy or sad? When Woody Allen was asked, "Are you afraid of death?" he said, "No, but I don't want to be there when it happens." That's a belief—believed in the gut but denied in the head. A mother dies after a long period of intense suffering, and some people in the family say, "God was somehow merciful to my mother, and this death saved her from all that pain and suffering." But another person in the same family says, "Suffering or not, she's my only mother, and I want her back as long as she can live and there is some hope." Someone else might say, "I have lost my mother on the physical level, but on the spiritual I will always have her. In fact, now that my mother is dead, she is more alive than when she was with us." Same death, same mother, same family, but different responses—it all depends on your beliefs.

What about failing an examination: is that good or bad, happy or sad? It all depends on your beliefs. For some, it is the end of their world and they con-
Beliefs are learned, and therefore they can be unlearned. template suicide, while for others it is a happy moment when they realize that their gifts and talents are calling them elsewhere, where they will be happier and more fulfilled. And still others look at the failure as an opportunity to learn from past mistakes and move on with their lives.

What about love? Is love good or bad, happy or sad? There is a story about a hospital administrator who visits the psychiatric ward of a hospital. A staff psychiatrist is giving him a tour. They come upon a man sitting with his head in his hands, rocking back and forth, and moaning over and over again, "Lulu, Lulu, Lulu." The administrator asks the psychiatrist about this man, and the psychiatrist tells him that Lulu is the name of the woman who rejected the man. He couldn't take the rejection, so he went out of his head and now just sits there babbling, "Lulu, Lulu, Lulu" and never stops. *What a shame*, thinks the administrator. The administrator and the psychiatrist continue their tour of the ward and come upon another man sitting with his head in his hands, rocking back and forth, and moaning, "Lulu, Lulu, Lulu" over and over again. The administrator asks the psychiatrist, "Did Lulu reject this one, too?" The psychiatrist says, "No, Lulu married this one."

There are those who believe that their happiness depends on the people who love them, while others believe that when someone loves them, that person does not make them happy but makes them aware of the source of their happiness within them. So if your loved one rejects you or just goes away or dies, that person does not take away your happiness.

Shakespeare wrote in *Hamlet*, "There is nothing either good or bad, but thinking makes it so." Our perception of situations in life will make us feel the way we feel, and these feelings will trigger certain behaviors. If we want to change the way we behave or our negative feelings or our self-imposed limitations that are blocking our experience of a big God, we need to work on our perception of life and our gut beliefs. We need to stop listening to the reactions of others that feed these learned beliefs and start freeing our perceptions and changing our beliefs.

40 Bible and Land

Archbishop Desmond Tutu once said that when the missionaries first came to Africa, they had the Bible, and the Africans had the land. The missionaries then said, "Let us pray." The Africans closed their eyes, and when they opened them, they had the Bible, and the missionaries had the land. In addition to having a literal meaning, Bible and land here are symbols. The Bible is the belief system from which we make meaning. And the land? The Africans were intimately linked to the land. It gave them their identity. It defined them as individuals and as tribes. So when the land was taken away from them, they became less themselves.

In our own lives, we have been given bibles of all kinds, and our land has been taken away from us. Because of the bibles we carry, we do not live full lives. One of the bibles we have is our parents' bible. Can you still hear your parents saying, "Girls never . . . ; boys always . . ."? I know a young woman in India whose mother drilled it into her that only her dead body would leave the home of her husband. Her marriage was arranged to a man who has a girlfriend. Soon after the wedding, he got his wife pregnant so she would not leave him. While he remained committed to the other woman, he would taunt his wife, saying the child she was carrying was not his. He keeps his wife as a servant to take care of the house and his parents. Now, the wife has a master's degree and is the only daughter of parents who are in the diplomatic services of the country. And yet, her mother's voice echoes loud and clear: *Only your dead body will leave the home of your husband.* The wife has attempted suicide three times but continues to live at the house of her husband.

Your family bible perhaps gave you your self-concept and defined the way you relate with different groups of people. When you reached the age of reason, you were taken to church and taught what to believe. The remarks of your teachers and your peers still echo in your subconscious being.

In our own lives, we have been given bibles of all kinds, and our land has been taken away from us.

Your spouse brought another bible into your life. The media, of course, gives you bibles that influence so many of your decisions. Think of how often you are told to "just do it." You are saddled with all these bibles—so whose life are you living? Where is your land? The only way to get your life back is to give away all your bibles, take back your land, write your own scriptures, and take responsibility for your life.

Jesus said, "Unless you hate your father and mother and brothers and sisters and your own self, you cannot be my disciples." Jesus wants us to know freedom.

41 I Need the Love and Approval of Everyone—a Damaging Root Belief

eliefs are learned, unlearned, and replaced by new beliefs. When it comes to triggering behavior, there are three root beliefs that we need to consider, as these tend to be the cause of most of our problems. The first root belief is that to be worthwhile, I must get the love and approval of everyone, or I must be perfect in everything I do. If I don't, I am useless and good for nothing, or I am worthless and feel anxious. Let me repeat this belief, because it is important: *I must get the love and approval of everyone, I must be perfect in everything I do; otherwise, I am worthless and feel anxious.*

What is unhealthy or irrational about this statement? I equate my self-worth with rejection, criticism, and failure. *I must get the love and approval of everyone; I must be perfect in everything I do.* The irrational words are *must, everyone,* and *perfect.* Now, what is a more rational way of saying this? What are some phrases that I could substitute for "I must"? How about "I would like," "It is desirable," "I wish I could get" the love and approval of everyone? But even if you desire or wish to be very, very good at everything you do, to get the love and approval of everyone—is that realistic or possible? No, it's not possible to get the love and approval of everyone. Is it *necessary* to get the love and approval of everyone? No, it is not necessary. Is it necessary to get the love and approval of significant people in my life—my parents, my spouse, or my children? Well, this is easier said than done.

Part of what causes my unhappiness is the demand I place on myself to get love from the people who are significant in my life. In a way, I am putting my happiness in their hands. My parents are going to be the ones who determine my happiness. If they love me, I'll be happy. If they reject me, I will be unhappy. It is the same with my spouse. If he or she loves me, then I'll be happy. If he or she doesn't love me, then I am going to be miserable. And it is the same with my children, or my boss, or my friends and companions. I need to get their love and approval to be happy; if I don't, then I feel anxious and worthless. What if someone criticizes me, says something mean and negative about me, or tells me there is something really wrong with me? I begin to feel nervous, anxious, and think, *Maybe that person is right about me.*

Here's the tricky part, the part that's a little difficult to accept. The truth is I don't need the love and approval of others, not even those whom I love, in order to be a full and worthwhile human being. Now, it would be nice—it would be wonderful, in fact—and very desirable to get the love and approval of parents, family, and those near and dear to me. But there is no universal law that says that unless I get the love of these people, I cannot be happy. I can still be happy. I can still know joy and satisfaction and lead a fully alive life. Yes, it's bad that my parents don't want me. It's bad that my parents died, or abandoned me when I was small, or that my childhood was a chaotic mess. It's bad that my spouse wants to divorce me or my child rejects me. But these things don't mean I cannot be happy. I can, because I am not the "me" that changes with the transitoriness of life: I am not the abandoned child; I am not the divorcé. I can be happy because I am the constant "I," created in the image and likeness of God, whose identity is in the Divine, in an unconditionally loving and cherishing God: "My beloved, I am pleased with you, my favor rests on you, my delight is in you." Children may need love; what adults need is to become loving people.

This root belief that we need others' love and approval is often difficult to change, especially for those who have had a sad or troubled past. It's true that our past influences our present, but it doesn't control our present or determine our future. The control is in our hands. We can change. I can make change happen in my life. My past experience may be having an influence on me today, but it need not control me right now or determine my future. Now, is it easy to reclaim control of my present or make change happen when my situation is being influenced by the past or by some person whom I love? Is it easy? No, it certainly is not. But is it impossible? It may be difficult, but it's not impossible, and I can do it if I want to do it.

I can take my life into my hands and make of it what I want to make of it. I do not have to be saddled with the belief that I need the love and approval of others. Just think about this. I may be loved by some and not by all; I may succeed in some things but not in everything; but ultimately, who am I? God's image and likeness, the divine breath.

Others Must Be Fair and Kind to Me— Another Root Belief

42

The second cause of a lot of our problems is the root belief that others must be fair and kind to us. *Others must be fair and kind to me; otherwise, they are useless and good for nothing, and I feel angry.* What do I mean by this? Just as Moses had the Ten Commandments, I have my own commandments written in stone, and God help those who break any of them, for I will judge those people and condemn them as worthless humans.

I have commandments when I believe, for example, that parents must always be good to all their children . . . A good parent must always be a good role model at home . . . A good parent never does this or that or whatever . . . A good child must always respect his or her elders . . . A good child never lies . . . A good boss is always fair and never unjust . . . A good friend is always there for me when I need him or her . . . A good friend is always a friend of my friends and an enemy of my enemies, likes those whom I like and dislikes those whom I dislike.

Whenever anyone breaks one of my commandments, I downgrade his or her worth as a human being and feel angry. I feel angry because I am making irrational demands on that person. The idea that a good friend or a good companion or a good spouse should always be there for me when I need help is irrational when it is a demand or an expectation and not a desire. It is also irrational to equate behavior with self-worth. The person with whom I am angry is still the image and likeness of the Divine, the very breath of God. *This*, not the person's behavior, is the basis of his or her self-worth. We hardly admit this when we're angry, but at least we can see people as what I like to call FHBs. An FHB is a fallible human being, who has a right to make mistakes—even very bad ones. When you are angry with someone, just tell that person that he or she is an FHB, and leave the person to spend days and perhaps sleepless nights trying to figure it out.

Anger is a ridiculous emotion. Think about it. The people I am angriest with are usually having a great time. They seem to be blessed more and more by life. I believe that God will punish them eventually, but their lives only get better. I try to convince myself that God is taking them high up in life only so that they will have a great fall. And yet nothing like this ever happens. The only one who suffers from my anger is me.

Additionally, I become more ridiculous in anger. I think about this person I am angry at when I wake up, and I feel his or her presence at the breakfast table. I leave my breakfast unfinished and rush off to my workplace, and this person's presence, my angry idea of him or her, follows me there. I may inflict this angry feeling onto my co-workers or even my friends or clients. If I decide to go to the movies that evening, I find the person I am angry with sitting right next to me, and half the movie is over and I have not been able to follow the story. And then, of course, I bring this person to bed with me, and I toss and turn the whole night, feeling his or her presence in my own bed. See how ridiculous anger is?

And <u>maybe</u>, just maybe, the thing <u>I am most upset about in another is something I have not reconciled within myself.</u>

Is there an alternative to anger? Remember that others cannot make me feel the way I do. Emotions are a choice, and so by applying the PQR formula (pause, question, respond), I can choose a proactive response. In questioning the situation, I realize that I am the one who is going to be negatively affected by my angry feelings, and so in my enlightened self-interest (which is another word for selfishness), I decide to be assertive.

St. Ignatius offers a model for assertive behavior in *The Spiritual Exercises*. The first step is to find a good interpretation for what the other person is saying or doing. It might be good to see the hurtful behavior as coming from either ignorance or unconscious pain. If I believe that the behavior is more deliberate, then St. Ignatius encourages me to take the second step of clarifying that deliberateness with the other person. There are three ways of doing this: I can ask the person what he really means by what he is saying or doing, or I can tell him how I feel when he says or does something that seems hurtful, or I can tell him what I would like from him.

> *The person with whom I am angry is still the image and likeness of the Divine, the very breath of God. This, not the person's behavior, is the basis of his or her self-worth.*

If that does not seem to work, then St. Ignatius offers the third step, which is to correct the person's behavior with kindness and love—to use every appropriate means to help the other person, his or her life and well-being, while doing something constructive with his or her negative behavior. In other words, I take his lemons and make lemonade. I love him and love him and love him. Sometimes—more often than one might think—this love will motivate the person to change his or her behavior. But I know that not everyone will change; this is irrational and why the root belief that people must be fair and kind to me is so dangerous. This is where freedom comes in; even if the person doesn't change, I remain a free and loving person—not an angry, resentful one—by responding assertively.

Assertive behavior leaves the doors of communication open, offers an alternative to anger, and might also help preserve friendships or even develop new ones.

Life Must Make Things Easy for Me—a Third Harmful Root Belief

43

L et's examine one more damaging belief: life must make things easy for me. *Life must make things easy for me; otherwise, life is not worth living, and I feel cheated or depressed.* Now I am making demands on life. It cannot rain. It cannot snow. It cannot be too hot. It cannot be too cold. The trains have to be on time. There cannot be an accident on the highway that makes me late. When my demands are not met, I feel that life is not worth living. I feel cheated and depressed. Sickness, death—there are many things in life that are not easy or fair. Life is not fair. But still I hold on to the belief that life must make things easy for me.

Swami Chinmayananda was once flying from Bombay to Delhi for a scheduled appearance. As the plane approached Delhi, the pilot came on the intercom and announced that the control tower had instructed him to circle the city: there was poor visibility because of fog and pollution, and the flight crew was to wait for further instructions. After ten minutes of this, the plane was sent back to Bombay. In the Bombay lounge, the people who had been on the plane were huffing and puffing about the Indian airlines. They compared them with foreign companies and blamed the Indian government for causing all the country's problems.

While this was going on, Swamiji had a comfortable seat and was happily reading notes that some of his devotees had sent him. Someone came up to him and asked him if he wasn't upset that they were sitting in Bombay when they had to be in Delhi. Swamiji chuckled and said that for the first time, Indian Airlines would take him to Delhi and back for the price of one ticket. He was very happy. Swamiji realized that it was no use feeling upset, because nothing could be done about the weather. If they took another plane, it would run into the same weather conditions and also be unable to land.

The question is this: if the plane did not land in Delhi that day, should Swamiji feel sad for the people who took the trouble to come out to listen to him and would return disappointed after singing a few devotional songs? A little bit, yes. If there was a businessman on that plane, and he lost a million dollars because he did not reach Delhi that day, should he be disappointed? A little bit, yes. If there was a doctor on that plane, and because she could not make it to Delhi one of her patients died, should she be depressed? A little bit, yes. But throwing up our hands and deciding that life is not worth living when things do not go according to our plan is a small-minded response to life.

We can try and try to control what happens to us, but some things are just beyond our control. The following story told by Anthony de Mello illustrates this:

Once upon a time, there was an alligator stuck in a net by a lakeside. A little boy passed by the lakeside, and the alligator called out to him, saying, "Will you please save my life and get me out of this net?" The boy looked at the alligator hesitatingly, and the alligator said, "You know, I look very frightful, but I am a mother, and if I die, my babies will also die, so please save my life." The little boy thought about the babies for a moment and then decided to save the alligator. As he freed her from the net, the alligator caught the boy in her large teeth. The startled boy cried, "What are you doing?!" And the alligator replied, "I've got to feed my babies now." The boy said, "Feed your babies?! I try to save your life, and this is what you do to me?" The alligator said, "Sorry, kid, but it is the law of life." "Law of life, my foot," he said. To which the alligator replied, "Ask anybody."

Now, there was this little bird sitting in a tree watching the whole thing unfold, so the two asked the bird, and the bird answered, "Two years ago, I had three little babies in the nest, and as I was coming back to the nest with some food for my babies, a snake crawled up the tree and into the nest. He ate my babies right in front of me while I was screaming and shouting at him. The alligator is right; it is the law of life."

The boy looked at the alligator and said, "Give me one more chance." The alligator said, "Fine, okay." So they asked a donkey walking by, and the donkey said, "Well, you know, when I was young, my master beat me up and got a lot of work out of me, mistreated me, did not feed me enough. And now that I am old, he has left me out here in the jungle, and one of these days a wild animal will come and eat me. The alligator is right; it is the law of life."

The boy couldn't believe his luck, so he pleaded, "One last chance—please." And the alligator relented. "Okay."

Now, lucky for the little boy, there was a rabbit hopping by that had probably been a Jesuit in his previous life. So they asked the rabbit, and the rabbit paused and then said, "Well, let's discuss the law of life." Reluctantly, the alligator agreed. The rabbit said to the alligator, "But first, you must let the boy go so that he can take part in our discussion. If you have him in your mouth, how can he participate?" The alligator looked at the rabbit, and the rabbit said, "Come on—look at the size of you, and look at the boy." So the alligator let the boy out of her mouth. Suddenly, the rabbit shouted, "Run!" and the boy ran and ran and ran, until he met up with the rabbit in the middle of the forest. After thanking the rabbit for saving his life, the boy sat with the rabbit for a minute to catch his breath. Then the rabbit asked the boy, "Your people still eat alligators, don't they? And that alligator is still partially caught in the net. I mean, you really didn't free the alligator completely. Why don't you go and tell your village before the alligator finishes the job?"

And that's what he did. He told the villagers, and that night the village had a big banquet of alligator. The boy and the rabbit were enjoying the celebration together, and the boy was so grateful to the rabbit for having saved his life. Then the boy's dog came up beside him, spotted the rabbit, and chased after him. The boy chased after the dog, screaming and shouting for it to heel, but he was too late. The dog caught the rabbit, broke its neck, and killed it. What did the boy say? "Well, I guess that alligator was right; it is the law of life."

Many things in life are beyond our control. We can do very little about the weather, natural calamities, sickness, and so many things that happen in our lives. Often we see these things as hardships, as unfair situations. But we do have the power to decide how we will respond to situations beyond our control. One effective response is the Serenity Prayer: "Lord, give me the serenity to accept the things I cannot change, the courage to change the things I can, and the wisdom to know the difference." Or we may use the Eastern way of looking for the divine presence in the unexpected. The Bible begins by telling us that in the beginning there was chaos and confusion all over the world, and God hovered over this chaos and out of it brought forth a new and beautiful creation. When my life is chaotic and I find it difficult to understand what is happening, let me allow the divine spirit to hover over my darkness, and let me wait for the new and the beautiful to spring forth in my life. Chaos is often the shortest path to our spiritual core.

44 The Man and the Caterpillar

This is a story about change that one of my students shared with me a few years ago. Later I learned it was from the wonderful novel *Zorba the Greek*, by Nikos Kazantzakis.

A man fell in love with a caterpillar, and every morning he would go and watch it. Any spare time he had he would spend with the caterpillar, simply watching it. One day, the caterpillar formed a cocoon, and the man couldn't wait for it to change into a butterfly. He watched and watched, and even got a little impatient. After several mornings, there was movement in the cocoon, and the man knew that soon the caterpillar would change into a butterfly. He saw the little head poking out of the cocoon, and it was beautiful. But the caterpillar was struggling within its cocoon, and the man felt sorry for it. He thought he would help the caterpillar who was becoming a butterfly, so he broke open the cocoon, and the butterfly dropped to the ground, unable to fly. Part of the process for a caterpillar to become a butterfly is exercising its wings within its cocoon. This lets the wings grow strong enough for the butterfly to fly.

Change is not a miracle. Change doesn't just happen. We have to make it happen. We have to work at it—but it is not always difficult. In fact, sometimes it is so easy that we don't believe that it's possible, we don't believe that we can change. The Buddha is supposed to have said that change is as easy as flipping a coin to the other side. What I believe is that if you want to change, you will change.

Change is not a miracle. Change doesn't just happen. We have to make it happen.

Maybe you are a little skeptical, and you feel like the wife and mother who went on a weekend workshop retreat and came back and told her family, "I had such a great weekend. I had breakthrough experiences. I gained all these wonderful insights." Then, looking at her family, she said, "But what's the use? None of you have changed."

If you really do experience change, trust that your family will change toward you, and if you truly embody the change, the world will change with you.

45 God Does Not Interfere

There are many things that happen in life that are beyond our control, like sickness, suffering, aging, and death. There are many things that happen in life that God does not interfere in. God has given us a certain freedom. God has given us free will. God will not interfere with our life. This is part of the law of life. We can pray that God will give us the strength to cope with whatever is going on, but most of the time our situations do not change. There is a law of life, and this is part of the mystery of suffering.

What is the meaning of this? What is the meaning of death? What is the meaning of suffering? What is the meaning of pain? What is the meaning of life? We know that one way we can find meaning is by saying that these things are God's will, that this is all a part of God's plan. Another way is in simply seeing that there is life and death, and suffering is part of it all. Pain is a part of life, and we learn to find meaning in pain and to work through pain. We cannot work around pain; we have to work through it. We have to work through it and make it work for us. This too is freedom. The Buddhists believe that pain that is not resisted purifies and enlightens; pain that is resisted becomes suffering. Pain enlightens us about the true meaning of life.

Do you know the famous story of the boy who bought a new bicycle and rode it to see the *Titanic* leave port on its maiden voyage? He was so excited by the *Titanic* and caught up in the celebration that he forgot his new bike and went home by the bus, as he usually did. When he reached home, he realized he had left his bicycle behind. He thought, *Somebody must have stolen it by now.* He took a taxi back to the port, and there was his bicycle, alone on the cycle stand, and he began thanking and praising God for having taken care of it. On his way home, he passed by a church and went inside to thank God personally. When he came out, the bike was gone.

God is not your watchman. God is not your security man. If you trust God, lock up your bike. If you trust God, lock up your house. God is not going to do for you and me what we can do for ourselves.

Consider the previous story about the man and the cocoon. The man tried to help the caterpillar that was becoming a butterfly get out of its cocoon, but he rushed the transformation process. The man who loved the butterfly saw its struggles, pitied it, and interfered. In the end, the butterfly fell to ground, unable to fly. If some person—or even God—interrupts the way life is unfolding for us, the process we are going through, before we are ready to accept help, we may not complete the change that is in progress. Or, at least, it will take us much, much longer. God is not going to do for you and me what we can do for ourselves, and most of the time, God does not intervene. God does not interfere.

> *God is not going to do for you and me what we can do for ourselves.*

46 When Are You Going to Die?

When are you going to die? Have you decided?

Strange question, isn't it? Can you plan your death? Has God decided when you are going to die? I don't know the answer to these questions, but I see a lot of things that make me wonder.

I have been with dying people in hospitals and in nursing homes, and I have ministered to the families of people who are dying. I have seen a dying person live longer than anyone expected, enabling loved ones to be at that person's bedside and spend those last precious moments with him or her. We've all probably heard of such stories. The doctor announces to the relatives of a dying person that the person has only a few days to live. Other loved ones are informed, and they rush to the bedside of the dying person. But after a month, the person is still alive. Then the family realizes that one of them isn't there, and so this missing loved one is told to come, that there's still time. The person arrives at the bedside of the man or woman who has been dying for weeks, and shortly afterward, the dying person lets go and dies.

I remember a woman I was called to visit because she had cancer. She had just come out of surgery, and the doctor had given her six months to live. I was meeting her for the first time, and one of her relatives introduced me, saying, "This is Paul from India, and he is a Jesuit priest." She looked at me and said, "You have a beautiful smile." I replied, "Thank you, but how are you?" "I'm fine," she said. I asked her, "What do the doctors say?" She answered, "The doctors don't know anything." She was eighty-eight years old at the time. She told me that she was going to live until she was ninety, and she did. I was there for her ninetieth birthday. People had come from all over, and here she was, having this grand celebration. I sat by her side and said, "Now that you are ninety, what's the plan?" She told me, "Well, I have two great-grandchildren who are on the way, and I want to enjoy them for a while—so I'm not going to die just yet."

Was God planning her death? No, she had a reason to live—there were great-grandchildren on the way. So along they came, and she was ninety-two, then ninety-three, maybe even ninety-four and still going strong. Then one of her daughters got cancer and was dying. The old woman told her daughter that she couldn't die before the old woman did. The old woman fell into a coma and was taken to the hospital. But still she didn't die. Why? One of her sons from California was coming to see her. When he showed up, he began to say a few prayers, and when he finished praying, she died.

Did God have anything to do with this? It's a question worth asking, and I don't have an answer, but I do want to think about it. How many people do you know or have you heard about who just die when they want to die? A friend of mine, a principal I knew in Bombay, chose not to get married so she could take care of her mother. She was very dear to her mother, and when her mother was taken to the hospital with an illness, my friend was there day and night to take care of her. She stepped out of the hospital for five minutes because she had something urgent to do. When she came back, her mother was dead. She felt guilty because she wasn't there when her mother died. I tried to tell her that, from my experience working in hospitals, this happens quite often: a person does not want to die in the presence of his or her loved ones. Step out for five minutes, and the person has the freedom to let go. It's not something to feel guilty about. In fact, he or she wants to spare you the pain.

This is another true story, about a Jesuit priest from Bombay. He had cancer and went to the hospital. When he was discharged, he told the administrator in charge, a nun, that the next time he came to the hospital, he would come to die. She said, "Father, go home and take your medication. Take care of yourself and pray for me, and I will pray for you. Now go." Six months later, he came back to the hospital with a briefcase and a cassock and said, "Remember what I told you? I have come to die." The doctor examined him and said the Jesuit didn't need to be hospitalized. But the sister said, "Admit him." She spoke with the priest, and he told her, "I am not going to die tonight." So she instructed the nurses that if the priest started to go, they were to call her, because she wanted to be by his bedside. The next morning, he woke up. He took a shower, put on his cassock, arranged his briefcase, rang the bell for the nurse, and asked her to lower his bed, as he was ready to die. The nurse said, "Wait!" She ran to call the sister, but by the time the sister arrived at his bedside, the priest was dead. Did God have a hand in this? Maybe, but this Jesuit definitely decided when he was going to die.

Some sneer at Anthony de Mello, saying that a man who taught people to relax could not relax himself and died of a massive heart attack at age fifty-six. The fact is that a year before he died, Anthony de Mello wrote to a friend to say that he had done what he was supposed to do in this life, and it was now time for him to pass on.

Then there's my mother. She had a great devotion to St. Anthony of Padua, for whom the number thirteen was very significant. My mother was born on June 13, and she was unconscious for about a week before she passed . . . on November 13. My father, on the other hand, told me years before he died that he wanted to die when he was eighty-six, and he did.

When are you going to die, and how much will your perception and experience of God influence the moment of your death?

When are you going to die, and how much will your perception and experience of God influence the moment of your death?

Your answer will certainly affect how you live now, so it's something to ask yourself and think about.

47 The Breath of God

One Sunday morning a couple of summers ago, I was in Shreveport, Louisiana, concelebrating Mass. While a former Baptist pastor preached, I was gripped with the thought of the breath of God. I spent the rest of that Eucharist wondering what the breath of God was like and what it meant for me to be the breath of God.

As I walked into the sacristy after Mass, a four-year-old named Neil walked up behind me and chirped, "Hi!" While I greeted Neil, his mother walked up behind him to say hello to me and tell me what little Neil had prayed at Mass that morning: "Jesus, please make my mom and dad good people. They are very bad!" I asked Neil if that was true, and he nodded his little head emphatically. After I asked Neil to pray for me as well when he prayed for his mom and dad, he asked me, "Father Paul, what did you pray for?" I knew what I had prayed for: the breath of God! But how was I going to tell little Neil that was my prayer? How would he understand? And so I said, hesitatingly, "I prayed that I would see God as God is." And Neil responded, "Is that all you prayed for?" I went on, "You know, Neil, when you see God's face, you do not need to pray for anything else." With that, little Neil took off to get himself some cookies, while I continued to visit with Neil's wonderful parents.

The following evening, Neil's mother met me at a celebration. She could not wait to share with me what had happened that morning. At breakfast, Neil got out of his toddler seat and came over to his mom, plopped himself on her lap, took her face in his tiny hands, and, looking into her eyes, said, "Mom, I can see God in you, and he is a girl."

Little Neil got it! He knew instinctively what the breath of God was all about. The Divine can be deeply experienced at any age; we need only allow ourselves the eyes to see and the ears to hear. As Jesus prayed, "I thank you, Father, for keeping these things from the wise and revealing them to little children."

The Divine can be deeply experienced at any age; we need only allow ourselves the eyes to see and the ears to hear.

48 Are You Running for Fun or for Your Life?

I once heard this fable about a dog who entertained himself by running after other animals. He would often boast about his great speed. He claimed that he could catch anything he chased. But one day his boastful claim was put to the test by a rabbit hopping by. The dog chased the rabbit, trying to catch it just to prove himself. But the rabbit outran the dog, while all the other animals laughed at the boastful hound.

The truth of the story is this: the dog was running for fun, and the rabbit was running for his life. In our lives, we need to ask ourselves if we are living every moment as fully as we can or if we are just drifting through a meaningless existence. We need to ask ourselves this—and often.

Is God your steering wheel in life or just your spare tire?

St. Paul is a good example for us. After his experience on the road to Damascus, St. Paul claimed that he did not waste his time looking at the past but strained forward to the upward call in Christ Jesus, ever deepening his relationship with the Divine (Philippians 3:13–14). He proclaimed, "I no longer live, but Christ lives in me" (Galatians 2:20).

St. Ignatius said that God is longing to show us who we really are. So is God your steering wheel in life or just your spare tire? Are you running for thrills, or are you running for your life? How much do you desire union and communion with God? All it really takes is the will to experience the Divine. Do you believe this?

I Hope You Make It, Kid

It was the 1984 Summer Olympics. The media covered many of the great athletes, but at the time the focus was on one, Carl Lewis, who was expected to break a sixteen-year-old record in the long jump, held by Bob Beamon. In one of the commercials that ran during the Games, Beamon said: "Back in the Olympic Games of 1968, I set a world record in the long jump. At the time, some people said no one would ever jump that far again. Well, over the years I've enjoyed sitting in front of my television set and watching them try. But now there's a new kid, I'm told, who might have a chance of breaking my record. Well, there's just one thing I have to say about that." People sat back, thinking they would hear yet one more arrogant proclamation, but Beamon's face brightened and he said, "I hope you make it, kid."

I hope you make it, kid.

I really do.

I hope you are blessed with an ever-bigger God and an ever-deeper journey into the divine life. I hope you question and reflect, listen and explore, trust and love. I hope you *live*. As we continue to seek to experience the Divine ever more completely, I leave you with one thing. Try this for your personal reflection:

Jesus said that if we believe, we can do the same things he did. In fact, Jesus assured us that if we believe, we will do even greater things than he.

Acknowledgments

This book could not have been written without the dedicated efforts of so many who believed in me. I would like to express my gratitude especially to Marilyn Hebenstreit, who taped a large number of my workshops and programs; Marilyn Woods and Agnes Murphy, who transcribed the tapes; Gen Eiler, who has preserved all the originals; and Mary Kay Bonness, who helped put the oral transcripts into a written form.

I wish to thank everyone at my publisher, Loyola Press, especially associate publisher Terry Locke and staff theologian Jim Campbell, who were the first to see potential in me after attending my workshops at the 2002 Ignatian Spirituality Conference and then hearing my keynote address at the 2005 conference. Thanks to Heidi Toboni, my developmental editor, who helped shape this book and shepherd it into being. To Heidi Hill, my talented copy editor; to Judine O'Shea, who facilitated my book's cover and interior design; and to Michelle Halm, my dedicated marketer and promoter. And special thanks must go to Joe Durepos, executive editor of acquisitions, who believed in my gifts, who sought with determination to bring me to Loyola Press as an author, and who spent hours and hours reading through my writings and listening to my recorded talks in order to discern the best outline for this publication.

In addition to these, there are people too numerous to thank by name on these pages or who I wish to thank personally. You are all precious to me and are in my heart. But I cannot forget my siblings, Flory, Dora, and Savio, for their constant support and encouragement, and my nephew Kenric, who has taught me how to live the Christian and the mystical life by his own life and example. Lisbert D'Souza, my Jesuit superior and friend, has persistently encouraged me to share my thinking with the rest of the world. Elizabeth Ingenthron stayed close to me throughout, fine-tuning my writing and finding my voice behind the words.

Last but not least, I want to remember all my Hindu and Buddhist mystic friends who stayed around just long enough to challenge me to deepen my spiritual life and seek the deepest possible experience of the Divine. But most of all, this book is an expression of my journey with St. Ignatius of Loyola and my relationship with the person, life, and teachings of Jesus Christ.

About the Author

F r. Paul Coutinho, SJ, is an internationally recognized Ignatian scholar and speaker who brings an Eastern flavor to Western spirituality. A native of India and a Jesuit from the Bombay province, he frequently leads retreats, gives spiritual direction, and trains people to lead the Spiritual Exercises. He holds master's degrees in both clinical psychology and religious studies, and he has a doctorate in historical theology from Saint Louis University, where he specialized in Ignatian spirituality and is now a visiting lecturer. Coutinho is currently the editor of *Ignis*, the South Asian Ignatian spirituality journal, and he serves as the director of Ignatian Spirituality Programmes for South Asia. He divides his time between India and the United States.

For more information about Paul Coutinho's books, DVDs, and products, or if you are interested in hosting a speaking engagement or a retreat by Fr. Coutinho, please call Loyola Press at 800-621-1008, or visit www.LoyolaPress.com /PaulCoutinho.

Also by Paul Coutinho, SJ

Ever feel like you'll never be good enough for God? Tired of trying to "get right" with the Divine through your own efforts? In *Just as You Are*, Paul Coutinho, SJ, addresses these common feelings of spiritual inadequacy— and shows us how God already loves each of us and simply asks that we embrace this amazing love and live in it on a daily basis.

Filled with thought-provoking stories, inspiring anecdotes, and memorable metaphors, *Just as You Are* makes clear that falling in love with the Divine is the only "work" we ever need to do.

Available through your local bookstore or by ordering direct.

800-621-1008
www.loyolapress.com/store

$18.95 • Hc • 2721-9

LOYOLAPRESS.
A JESUIT MINISTRY

Beyond the Book . . .

How Big Is Your God? video

This 15-minute video features Paul Coutinho, SJ, leading a retreat where he addresses some of the topics from *How Big Is Your God?* To view this video, please visit **www.loyolapress.com/coutinho-retreat**

How Big Is Your God? and *Just as You Are*

by Paul Coutinho, SJ, are now available as eBooks. Visit **www.loyolapress.com** to purchase these other formats.

Ignatian Spirituality Online

Learn more about prayer, spiritual direction, retreats, and how to make good decisions at **www.ignatianspirituality.com**